YoungWriters

GW01374900

ONCE UPON A RHYME

POEMS FROM THE EAST

Edited by Donna Samworth
& Claire Tupholme

First published in Great Britain in 2011 by:

Young Writers

Remus House
Coltsfoot Drive
Peterborough
PE2 9BF
Telephone: 01733 890066
Website: www.youngwriters.co.uk

All Rights Reserved
Book Design by Tim Christian
© Copyright Contributors 2010
SB ISBN 978-0-85739-324-1

THIS BOOK BELONGS TO

....

Foreword

Here at Young Writers our objective is to help children discover the joys of poetry and creative writing. Few things are more encouraging for the aspiring writer than seeing their own work in print. We are proud that our anthologies are able to give young authors this unique sense of confidence and pride in their abilities.

Once Upon a Rhyme is our latest fantastic competition, specifically designed to encourage the writing skills of primary school children through the medium of poetry. From the high quality of entries received, it is clear that Once Upon a Rhyme really captured the imagination of all involved.

The resulting collection is an excellent showcase for the poetic talents of the younger generation and we are sure you will be charmed and inspired by it, both now and in the future.

Contents

Maddie Stewart is our featured poet this year. She has written a nonsense workshop for you and included some of her great poems. You can find these in the middle of your book.

Carys Slater (6) 1

Bentley Primary School, Ipswich
Toby Schofield (7) 1
Tom Pepper (10) 2
Alex Christison (10) 2
James Bailey (11) 3
Oliver Christison (8) 3
Harry Rampling (10) 4
Craig Annis (9) 4
Megan Edevane (7) 5
Will Cooper (10) 5
Eloise Prior (9) 6
Harriet Schofield (9) 6
Caitlin Edevane (9) 7
Emiline McCart (9) 7
Harry Prior (8) 8
Lucia Callis (9) 8
Tollef Geelmuyden (8) 9
Thalia (7) 9

Brookside Junior School, Romford
Dammy Ogunlade (9) 10
Maisie Cates (10) 10
Michael Whippy (9) 11
Paige Axten (9) 11
Sydney Webster (9) 12
Tommy William Gard (9) 12
Mari Preka (9) 13
Katie Louise Conway (9) 13
Tia-Leigh Reeve (9) 14

Tyler Spiers (9) 14
Megan Katie Price (9) 15
Harry JD Baker (9) 15
Jack O'Connor (9) 16
Aaron Wennington (9) 16
Jessica Empson (10) 17
Amy Lorraine Harvey (9) 17
Lucy May-Wallace (9) 18
Danny Harrop (9) 18

Crowfoot Community Primary School, Beccles
Maria Hill (7) 19
Paris Tomlinson Womack (8) 19
Tamzin Wright (8) 20
Anya Sainsbury (8) 20
Zara Alexander (8) 21
Tyler Copeman (8) 21
Thomas Read (8) 22
Thomas Bloomfield (8) 22
Tay Morey (8) 23
Suzi Robinson (8) 23
Stuart Moon (8) 24
Sarah Playford (8) 24
Millie Anderson (8) 25
Kyesha Gilham (8) 25
Kieran Hart (8) 26
Kate Alexander (8) 26
Isaac Coleman (8) 27

Harrison Wright (8) 27
Cerys Russell (8) 28
Callum Homes (8) 28

Duchy of Lancaster CE Methwold Primary School, Thetford
Ellie Giles (7) 29
Daniel Bailey (10) 29
Wil Doughty (9) 30
Ally-Jane Scott Stevenson (10) 30
Reuben Cocksedge (10) 31
Jazmine Rebecca Murray (10) 31
Lewis Bunten (10) 32
William Kimber (9) 32
Kia Byrne (9) 33
Evie Chaplin (9) 33
Olivia Rodwell (8) 34
Ana Robertson (7) 34
Raith Bailey (7) 35
Abbi Bartrum (8) 35
Jessica Meehan (8) 36
Willow King (7) 36
Catherine Louise Parker (8) 37
Jaime Ramsay (7) 37
Jessica Webb (8) 38
Katie Manning (7) 38
Jamie Vowles (8) 39
Katherine Woods (9) 39
Caitlin Daisy Jupp (8) 40
Elizabeth Rose Cocksedge (8) 40
Megan Ann Hamilton (9) 41
Bonnie Mary Barber (7) 41
Callum West (9) 42
Maddison Skye Bunten (7) 42
Brennan Scott Stevenson (7) 43
Rhiannon Weatherley (9) 43
Imogen Rose Pick (8) 44
Jasmine Bunten (8) 44
Kaleise Bunten (8) 45
Thomas Harper (11) 45
Grace Howse (9) 46
Harry Butcher (9) 46
Jenna Ramsey (9) 47

Edward Worlledge Community Junior School, Great Yarmouth
Jasmine Loades (7) 47
Chloe Smith (7) 48
Harvey Faraday Drake (7) 48
Tia Williams (7) 49
Misha Marjoram (7) 49
Kayley Nash (7) 50
Parys Green (7) 50
Ben Brown (8) 51
Chelsea Glover (7) 51
Bethany Coulson (7) 52
Dylan Ward (7) 52

Gearies Junior School, Ilford
Shenel Mushtaq (10) 53

Hadleigh Junior School, Benfleet
Harriet Smith (8) 53
Summer Hall (11) 54

Hardwick Primary School, Bury St Edmunds
Benjamin Foreman (8) 54
Olivia Lingwood (8) 55
Chloe Sparks (8) 55

Hartest CE VC Primary School, Bury St Edmunds
Chanel Healy (8) 56
Zara Smith (8) 56

Heycroft Primary School, Leigh-On-Sea
Michael Oxby (9) 57
Tigi Whitehouse (9) 57
Summer Hurley (9) 58
Kloe Snowdon (9) 58
Daniel Seaman (9) 59
Morgan Woodward (9) 59
Luke Collins (9) 60
Mason Wakeling (10) 60
Emma Partner (9) 61
Isobel Dowden (10) 61
Ellise Pratt (9) 62
Will Fenton (9) 62
Jessica Hawes (9) 63
Star Bewley (9) 63
Chloe Nall (10) 64

Joe Haines (9) 64
Creág MacDonald (10) 65
Dean Morriss (9)....................................... 65
Ryan Brooks (9) 66
Christopher Ho (9)..................................... 66
Thomas Barnard (9) 67
Darcie Catling (9) 67
Maisie Spicer (9) 68
Oliver Towning (10).................................... 68
Joseph Barnard (9) 69
Tom Cracknell (10) 69
Thomas Gavriel (10).................................. 70
Michael Jones (9)...................................... 70
William Abbott (9) 71
Freya Morton (9)....................................... 71
Alice Martin (9) 72
Alice Wise... 72
Alfie Taylor (9) 73
Katie Bourdillon (9).................................... 73

Hurst Primary School, Bexley
Jack Christie (10) 74
Tom Shea (10) 74
Ezrie Cornford (10) 75
Harry Powley (10) 75
Kyle Anthony David Brown (10) 76
Tegan Battersby (10) 76
Emily Jenson (10)...................................... 77
Ellie Owen (10) 77
Joe Williams (10) 78
Isabella Kane (10) 78
Eliane Newitt (10) 79
Jamie Mitchell (10) 79
Paige Bridger (10) 80
Lewis Watson (11)..................................... 80
Harrison Callard (10) 81
Jamie Lyons (10) 81
Brooke Connell (10) 82
Savannah Golesworthy (10)....................... 82
Joseph Hopper (11) 83
Emily Roffey (10) 83
Lauren Couldwell (10) 84
Ellie Lenzi (10) 84
Megan Sweeney (10) 85

Melisa Chakarto (10) 86
Maddie Wheale (10).................................. 87
Adam De Bolla (10) 87
Aqil Sabir (10)... 88
Ellie Badcock (11) 89
Georgina Doig (11) 90
Casey Jones (10) 90
Tendai Joshua Spicer (11)......................... 91
Fintan Murphy (10) 92
Miranda Parkin (10) 92
Suzanna Page (11) 93
Ahmed Negm (11)..................................... 94

Kingston Primary School, Benfleet
Charlotte Ing (11) 95
David Batchelor (10) 96
Thomas Elliott (10) 96
Lavinia Tidy-Jones (10) 97
James Hill (10) 97
Heather Marshall (11)................................ 98
Shaun Gayford (10)................................... 98
Shannon Burton (10) 99
Benjamin Rackley (10) 100
Joel Wright (11) 100
Sam Phillips (10) 101
Abigail Bush (10) 101
Sean Roe (10) 102
Sally Logan (10) 102
Christian Lister (10) 103
Jessica Mendies (10) 103
Joseph Greenwood (10) 104
Connor Wallington (10) 117
Reece McAnulty (10) 117
George Norris (10) 118

Magdalen Gates Primary School, Norwich
Jasmine Carrier (9).................................. 118
Niamh Canny (10) 119
Ruben Price (9) 119
Jordan Rhys Townsend (10).................... 120
Devon Dray (10) 120
Hannah Cooper (9) 121

Joe Kirman (9)	121
Mina Mitchell-Hardy (9)	122
Maia Kemp-Welch (10)	122

Newlands Primary School, Ramsgate
Michael Norton (10)	123
Summer Gadd (10)	123
Charlotte Shorter Coombes (10)	124
Oliver Annis (10)	124
Jack Taylor (10)	125
Cameron Sanham (11)	125
Olivia Martin (10)	126
Katie McCullough (10)	126
James Bennett (10)	127
Marcus Baldwin (10)	127
Cerys Haine (10)	128
Georgia Dooney (10)	128
Chelsea Usher (10)	129

Pickhurst Junior School, West Wickham
Cassandra Thatcher (9)	129
Isabelle Secord (9)	130
Henry Allen (10)	130
Stanley Mattless (9)	131

Queen's Hill Primary School, Norwich
Jacob Taylor-Green (10)	131
Ola Krukowka	132
Isobel Wilkinson	132
Megan White	133
Ebonhi Andrews (10)	134
Abi Lloyd (10)	134
Georgia Coulthard & Alyssa Newton	135

Redcastle Furze Primary School, Thetford
Addison Malkinson (9)	135
Byron Brown (9)	136
Max Dimon (9)	136
Joao Lampreia (9)	137
Ruby Dean (10)	137
Jordan Hampton (9)	138
Abby Fendley (9)	138
Levi Strutton (10)	139

Thomas Hazelden (9)	140
Krystina Davis (9)	141
Jazmine Louise Riley (9)	142

Roach Vale Primary School, Colchester
Lauren Bibby (10)	143
Luke Heffron (10)	144
Elise Jones (10)	144
Tommy McWhirter (10)	145
Harrison Goulding (10)	145
Charlie Robinson (10)	146
Dylan Abraham (10)	146
Kieran Phillips (10)	147

Rushmere Hall Primary School, Ipswich
Abigail Sample (7)	147
Melissa Neale (7)	148
Chloe Louise Last (7)	148
Jordan Campbell (7)	149
Mia Blackman (7)	149
Francesca Roberts (7)	150
Deimante Miceviciute (7)	150
Shalom Shibi (8)	151
Harriet Rush (8)	151
Emily Gallant (8)	152
Phoebe Dodd (8)	152
Eden Upson (8)	153
Kaylee Meekings (8)	153
Bobby Crowhurst (8)	154
Cameron Cornthwaite (8)	154
Jayden Novak (8)	155
Laura Towler (8)	155
Paige James (9)	156
Esha Khan (9)	156
Mashiat Anwar (9)	157
Manraj Digpal (9)	157
Melanie Sharpe (9)	158
Chloe Gordon (9)	158
Hannah Leek (9)	159
Sophie Campbell (9)	159
Prakash Modasia (10)	160
Imogen Clarke (11)	160
Tilly Crowhurst (10)	161

Jordan Flude (9) 162
Toby Ashbee (9) 162
Jonathan Ferris (9) 163

St Augustine of Canterbury Primary School, Gillingham

Abigail Page (11) 163
Jake Turner (10) 164
Kirsty Verrent (10) 164
Natasha Udu (10) 165
Amber MacGregor (10) 165
Ellie Harding (11) 166
Daisy Lukins (10) 166
Cheyenne Hepburn (11) 167
Bradley Williams (10) 167
Rachael Mancattelli (10) 168
June King (10) 168
Millie Nunn (10) 169
Isaac Owen (11) 169
Nathan Page (11) 170

St Augustine's CE Junior School, Peterborough

Ebony Cummins (7) 170
Natalia Hutchings (7) 171
Lauren Ippolito (7) 171
Lucy Royle (7) 172
Alfie Anderson (7) 172
Angel-Skye Hudson (7) 173
Ebonie Rhode (8) 174

St Lawrence CE Primary School, Colchester

Fearn Short (11) 174
Isabella Hutton (10) 175
Frank Bush (10) 175
Finley Hughes (10) 176
Chloe Tatum (9) 176
Holly Went (10) 177
Neave Lynes (11) 177
Jordan Moncur (10) 178
Cara Brackpool (10) 178
Sean Sargent (10) 179
Georgia Scott (10) 179
Ewan Black (10) 180
Jordan Mitchell (10) 180

Thomas Dunningham (11) 181
Megan Till (10) 181
Joshua Tatum (11) 182

The King's School, Ely

Katherine Mann (7) 182
Eleanor Wallace (8) 183
India Thomas (8) 183
Izzy McMillan (7) 184
Lucky Daniel Pogoson (7) 184
Jasmine Choudhry (9) 185
Bethany Thorpe (10) 186
Isabelle Jupp (8) 186
Aurora Segre Carnell (7) 187
Hannah Okechukwu (10) 188
Darcie Jupp (10) 189
James Hinton (10) 189
Katie Diss (10) 190

The Westborough School, Westcliff-on-Sea

Erin Ilma Carney (7) 192
Sharna Gosling (7) 192
Hollie Upton (7) 193
James Loughran (7) 103
Molly Tudor (7) 194

Welbourne Primary School, Peterborough

Anne-Marie Ewing (7) 194
Charlie Orbell (7) 195
Karis Adams (7) 196
Owen Reed (7) 197
Erikas Grigutis (7) 197
David Cruz (7) 198
Brandon Bonner (7) 198
Caery Brandreth (7) 199
Jacob Thompson 199
Daria Slaby (7) 200

Wicklewood Primary School, Wymondham

Mia Thomsett-Hurrell (10) 200
Thomas Marshall (10) 201
Kirstin Angus (10) 201
Katie Ellen King (10) 202
Molly Young (10) 202
Phoebe Burton-White (10) 203

Dominic Cohen (11) 203
Catherine Jones (10) 204
Rebekah Devlin (10) 204
Tonita Holloway (10) 205
Luke Custance (10) 205
Helena Imogen Geere (11) 206
Toby Dunn (8) 206
Maria Shepherd (10) 207
Harry Snook (10) 207
Anya Grace Droppert (10) 208
Owen Sully (10) 208
Lewis Saunders (8) 209
Samantha Osborne (9) 209
Ashley Bishop (10) 210

Worsley Bridge Junior School, Beckenham
Lauryn Peacock 210
Suzannah Ogunleye (10) 211
George Barrett (10) 211
Teyam Goode (10) 212
Sacha Shiels (10) 212
Max Owen (10) 213
Tyruss Mays (10) 213
Luke Lawrence (10) 214
Delaney Anne Brewster (10) 214
Chloe Brown (10) 215
Leah Purton (10) 216
Shannon Partleton (10) 216
Charley Anderson (10) 217
Mia Calver (10) 218
Danielle Allen (10) 218
Archie Palmer (10) 219

The Poems

What Am I?

These minibeasts can hide
They leave a trail
They are very friendly
You can get them in gardens
They like water
You can hold some
They don't have good eyesight
They can have babies
They are tiny
And there can be loads of them
There are loads in gardens
They like mud.

Snails.

Carys Slater (6)

World War II

The beautiful poppies blaze after the war
Planes soar through the air
Descending bombs fall, covering the smouldering sky.
The heroic soldiers viciously fight for victory.
Houses collapse everywhere
Children crying, smoke in the air, gas masks on.

Toby Schofield (7)
Bentley Primary School, Ipswich

The Courageous Soldiers

Guns cocked, armed and ready,
shooting bullets fast and heavy.

Snipers glitching here and there,
bullets shooting everywhere.

Rubble landing on the ground,
massive, deadly bombs spinning round and round,
just missing buildings, eventually hitting the ground.

Tom Pepper (10)
Bentley Primary School, Ipswich

Retreat!

Booming turrets, clanking tracks, *run! Run!*
It's the Gerry's tanks
Charging soldiers drawing near
We're running, leaping full of fear.

Camouflage colours blending in,
Watch out! Watch out!
They're hemming us in!

Spitfires zipping through the air,
Here, there and everywhere.
Bombs fire round and round,
Exploding as they hit the ground.
Move away, stay alive,
Let's hope the end is nigh.

Alex Christison (10)
Bentley Primary School, Ipswich

Fight For Dunkirk

Blood-splattered corpses thrown on the ground.
Fearful privates trying to be found.
Cold steel bullets whizzing near.
Blood-covered soldiers crying with fear.
Armed soldiers creeping in,
Holding a grenade, pulling out the pin.
Blood-splattered man he's my friend!
The angel of death, bringing me to my end.
No point in running away.
No point in trying again.

James Bailey (11)
Bentley Primary School, Ipswich

World War II

The remembrance of the red,
scarlet of the dead,
never forget the hope we had in that war.

Soaring, whizzing, zooming, dodging
thunderous, piercing noise coming from the sky.
Brave, fearless, courageous, heroic soldiers
marching through the town
screaming, shouting, shooting things down.
Collapsing buildings crumbling down, terrified cries,
smoke and explosions fill the sky.

Oliver Christison (8)
Bentley Primary School, Ipswich

The Blitz

With the planes swooshing though the air.
Bombs whistling straight into men killing them ten by ten.
Bullets shooting with no care
over here and over there.
People in an air-raid shelter
praying for their dad.
Hugging their mum, saying,
'I hope my dad does not die.'

Harry Rampling (10)
Bentley Primary School, Ipswich

Life Or Death?

Guns firing, deadly bullets causing pain and agony.

Turrets booming at the enemy,
Tank wheels clanking,
Squashing anything in their path,
Soldiers screaming upon the battlefield.

Wounded bodies, dragging themselves to safety,
Knifes dripping with enemy blood.

Missiles floating through the air,
People screaming everywhere,
A pile of bodies over there.

I closed my eyes and my mate died.

Craig Annis (9)
Bentley Primary School, Ipswich

World War II Poem

Scarlet poppies are gleaming in the field
We shall never forget
The planes were whizzing in the sky
Dropping bombs as they did fly
Blazing flames smouldering the sky
As the children did cry.

Megan Edevane (7)
Bentley Primary School, Ipswich

Live Or Die?

Blazing guns shooting through the smoky air.
Screaming bodies everywhere.
Thinking hard, knowing that death is near.
Thinking more brings a tear.
Shouted back to my mate.
Seeing him in his bloody state.

Turned back to see the tanks.
The explosions in the higher ranks.
The enemy is drawing in.
Grab the grenade, pull the pin.
Listening to the terrible bang.
Watching, waiting for the gang.
Will we live?
Will we die?
Closing my eyes and saying goodbye.

Will Cooper (10)
Bentley Primary School, Ipswich

A Doleful World War II Poem

Bullets whistling through the air,
Screaming people everywhere.

Dark green planes, circles of blue,
Spitfires heading straight for you.

Caterpillar tracks on the ground,
Germans trying to track them down.

Soldiers crying
Soldiers dying
Will this ever end?

Eloise Prior (9)
Bentley Primary School, Ipswich

Evacuation Poem

Steam train whistling loudly
As we leave the station.

Puff, puff down the track,
I will never ever look back.

The box is big, brown and heavy,
'Mummy, I want my teddy.'

Teddy, teddy don't be scared
Teddy, teddy, be prepared.

The war has finished
I am free
I'm going home to my family.

Harriet Schofield (9)
Bentley Primary School, Ipswich

Evacuation Poem

Puff, puff down the trail.
Waving goodbye and off we wail.

Teddy, teddy, come with me
Teddy, teddy, you smell like me.

Carry my box
Then I freeze
I saw my new parents
Then I burst into tears.
Would I see my parents again?

Caitlin Edevane (9)
Bentley Primary School, Ipswich

Survival

Guns firing, straight at you,
Zooming, whizzing, deadly and true!

Caterpillar tracks on the ground,
Freshly made, look around!

Dark green camouflage in the gloom,
Look out! Someone is looking at you!

Stabbing soldiers with their guns,
Hoping that tomorrow comes.

Emiline McCart (9)
Bentley Primary School, Ipswich

World War II

Red scarlet poppies are for remembering about the brave soldiers who save our lives.

Spitfire planes are whizzing around the world
descending bombs and defending the skies.

The soldiers didn't give up fighting the other team
because they didn't want to lose.
They were petrified.

The bombs hit all the buildings and St Paul's wasn't hit.
It is still here today.

Harry Prior (8)
Bentley Primary School, Ipswich

World War II Poem

The poppies are never forgotten and the colour is scarlet.
To remember the dead soldiers the poppies are exquisite.

The planes whizz through the skies.
The ghosting bombs drop on the building.
The children petrified in their shelter.

The ice-cold bodies frozen
Our brave soldiers never give up.

Smokey buildings slowly crashing to the ground
as the bombs explode everywhere.

Lucia Callis (9)
Bentley Primary School, Ipswich

World War II Poem

Red scarlet poppies are the brave heroic soldiers
who gave their lives for us.

Spitfires fly through the bullet-dodging sky
as they drop their bombs that descend in thousands.

The extraordinary heroic soldiers that fought for our lives.

Hear the sound of weeping children as bombs blow up
and buildings get crushed.

Tollef Geelmuyden (8)
Bentley Primary School, Ipswich

World War II Poem

Red is for poppies, never forget what the soldiers did.
Zooming planes through the sky, descending bombs as they fly.
Brave soldiers fearlessly fight all night,
Collapsing buildings exploding in the land.

Thalia (7)
Bentley Primary School, Ipswich

Metrostrijilin

Metrostrijilin is a very beautiful pet
She travelled right here in a private jet
I've never seen anything like it before
It scratches me with its big fat claw!
Metro likes to wear her cap
With her wings she flies; *flap, flap, flap!*
She lives in my pretty garden
She burps a lot and then says pardon
I love my pet, oh so much
Still when she flies away, we will never lose touch.

Dammy Ogunlade (9)
Brookside Junior School, Romford

JD

JD is a very creative pet,
He wants to join the Cadets,
I've never seen anything like it before,
He even brought his snowman indoors,
JD likes to eat snails,
So be careful he also likes to bite nails,
He likes to live in my shed
And he likes to play with his ted,
I love my pet so much
And he also speaks English and Dutch!

Maisie Cates (10)
Brookside Junior School, Romford

Mike

Mike is a lovely pet
He also has a jet
I've never seen anything like him before
He likes playing with my door
When he eats he makes gold
But it's all covered in mould
He likes his bed in my shed
He can't sleep without his ted
He's soft to touch
He also knows Dutch!

Michael Whippy (9)
Brookside Junior School, Romford

Danny

Danny is a very crazy pet
Animals teased him and he got upset
I've never seen him so sad before
Until he met a dinosaur
He taught him to play football
He bought some boots at the mall
He sleeps in his bed, in the shed
Not without his ted
I love him so much, he speaks Dutch
Animals don't tease him anymore.

Paige Axten (9)
Brookside Junior School, Romford

Billy

Billy is a very chatty pet
He likes to go on the internet
Billy always sees me as a threat
As I leave he seems to be free
His favourite musical is Glee
He loves to see me
He likes to say, 'Hey hee.'

Sydney Webster (9)
Brookside Junior School, Romford

Patrick Monster

Patrick Monster is a very ugly pet.
He lies in the sunset.
I've never seen anything like him before.
He smashed his head against the door.
He loves playing hockey.
He is very cocky.
He lives in the shed.
That he dreads.
He is nice to touch.
If he is naughty he goes in the hutch.

Tommy William Gard (9)
Brookside Junior School, Romford

Bob

Bob is a very bonkers pet
He will never be a good vet
I've never seen anything like it before
He always slams the door
He loves eyeballs
And climbs up the walls
He sleeps in a bed
In my own shed
I love him so much
He even speaks Dutch.

Mari Preka (9)
Brookside Junior School, Romford

Rose

Rose is a very wacky pet,
she is badly in debt.
I've never seen anything like it before
She's as big as a dinosaur!
But I like Rose and she likes her bed
which remains in my shed
She has bad dreams
which she dreads.

Katie Louise Conway (9)
Brookside Junior School, Romford

Cheeky

Cheeky is a very furry pet
Please do not get him wet
I've never seen anything like it before
He's bigger than a dinosaur
He street dances everywhere
He lives in a house
He isn't scared of a mouse
He loves to be in bed
And be fed
I love him so much
He's always in my clutch.

Tia-Leigh Reeve (9)
Brookside Junior School, Romford

Dopy

Dopy is a very wacky pet,
He'll never be a good vet,
I've never seen anything like it before,
When he goes out he slams the door,
Dopy likes to eat dog food
And he's always in the mood,
He lives in my house,
He screams when he sees a woodlouse,
I love my pet so much,
He speaks English and Dutch,
I love my pet Dopy.

Tyler Spiers (9)
Brookside Junior School, Romford

Jacky

Is a very athletic and sporty pet
Please do not get him upset
I've never seen anything like this before in my life
He is bigger than a T-rex
He snores so loud
He turns the house inside out.
He always lets out a big roar
I wake with a fright in the middle of the night
But it was a nightmare!

Megan Katie Price (9)
Brookside Junior School, Romford

Harry

Harry is a thick pet
My pet is a real threat!
I have never seen anything like it before
He jumped through the floor
He eats peanuts
He hates coconuts
He lives under the stairs
He hates big, bad bears
I love him so much
He's soft to touch.

Harry JD Baker (9)
Brookside Junior School, Romford

Steven Gerrard

Steven Gerrard is a very cool pet
Unfortunately he is bad at debt
I've never seen anything like it before
Bigger than a dinosaur
Stringer than a chainsaw
His favourite movie is 'Money for the Poor'
He lives in a massive shed
His favourite bed is named Fred
I love my pet and his friend Fred.

Jack O'Connor (9)
Brookside Junior School, Romford

Harry

Harry is a very funny pet
My pet is sad at sunset
I've never seen anything like it before
It likes to roar
My pet likes to fly
My pet likes to say bye
He lives in my house
He can't sleep without his mouse
I love my pet so much
He can even speak Dutch.

Aaron Wennington (9)
Brookside Junior School, Romford

Ugly Betty

Ugly Betty is a very weird pet
Animals teased her so she got upset
I've never seen her so sad before
Until she met a dinosaur
He taught her how to play football
So she bought some boots at the mall
She sleeps in a bed
but not without her ted
Animals don't tease her anymore
As she plays with a dinosaur
She celebrated with a plate of worms
Even if they had germs!

Jessica Empson (10)
Brookside Junior School, Romford

My Pet Mia

Mia is a very weird pet.
She's got a very bad leg, she needs a vet.
I've never seen anything like it before.
She always slams the door.
She likes to catch a ball with her tongue.
But she really hates lots of buns!
She lives in the shed
And she can't sleep without her ted.
I love her so much,
She's soft to touch!

Amy Lorraine Harvey (9)
Brookside Junior School, Romford

Rosetta

Rosetta is a lovable pet.
Please do not get her wet.
I have never seen anything like it before.
She always runs into the door.
But in her sleep she always lets out a big *roar!*
But she only likes raw food.
She lives in the shed.
But bad dreams she dreads.
And my pet loves new beds.
I love her so much I can't ever lose touch.

Lucy May-Wallace (9)
Brookside Junior School, Romford

Fred

Fred is a very crazy pet
My pet is a threat
I've never seen anything like it before
He's bigger than a dinosaur
He likes to sleep in a shed
With a ted.

Danny Harrop (9)
Brookside Junior School, Romford

In My Paradise

In my paradise I would see chocolate moons,
Candy rainbows and flower fairies that make my garden pretty.
I would see butterflies on my fingers, that's so special to me.

In my paradise I would be in dancing pictures painted by Picasso.
I would play music to the queen fairy,
the viola and the harp.
I would play piano to the pixies in the park.

In my paradise I'd have cute, fluffy kittens to play with
and teddies to cuddle tight.
I would have my family and friends to share my paradise.
This would be an amazing life.

Maria Hill (7)
Crowfoot Community Primary School, Beccles

A Beautiful Rose

I bloom in summer just from a seed
and I open as beautiful as the sun
I sit there and smile all day long
a snowflake drops and I shrivel, crackle and I die
But when summer is back It starts all over again.

Paris Tomlinson Womack (8)
Crowfoot Community Primary School, Beccles

I Am . . .

Funny as a Picasso painting.
Lively as a fox running in and out of its hole.
Loud as a clap of thunder shouting in a megaphone.
Silly as a monkey swinging from tree to tree.
Active as a rabbit jumping up and down with its floppy ears.

Tamzin Wright (8)
Crowfoot Community Primary School, Beccles

I Am . . .

As quiet as a mouse creeping towards some cheese.
As funny as a hippo wallowing in the mud.
As lively as a rabbit hopping across a field.
As cheeky as a monkey throwing nuts at the other animals.
As impatient as a rhino charging to get its food.
As playful as a puppy chasing its tail.
As cute as a newborn kitten sleeping on a roof.

Anya Sainsbury (8)
Crowfoot Community Primary School, Beccles

I Am . . .

Cheeky as a monkey in a tree throwing bananas
Funny as a clown throwing water bombs at his face
Happy as a sleepy rabbit in a bed
Noisy as a donkey yawning very long
Quiet as a family of mice in their bed
Friendly as a mole reading
Fabulous as an owl sleeping in daylight.

Zara Alexander (8)
Crowfoot Community Primary School, Beccles

I Am . . .

Cheeky as a monkey throwing a banana skin
Funny as a clown squeezing into a funny car
Loud as a band playing
Cool as a camel on the computer
Fast as a cheetah racing against a racing car.

Tyler Copeman (8)
Crowfoot Community Primary School, Beccles

I Am . . .

I am funny and I have two dogs
I wonder if Santa Claus is real
I hear dogs barking in the park
I see my dog Gem jumping for the ball
I want a scrambler bike
I am funny and I have two dogs
I feel happy
I worry about nothing
I want a scrambler bike
I try to ride a scrambler bike
I hope to find a land of chocolate one day
I am funny and I have two dogs.

Thomas Read (8)
Crowfoot Community Primary School, Beccles

I Am . . .

As funny as a monkey throwing bananas at the zookeeper
As speedy as a zooming car going down the road
As pretty as Mum wearing a pretty dress
As cheeky as a cheetah running in a jungle.

Thomas Bloomfield (8)
Crowfoot Community Primary School, Beccles

I Am . . .

Fast as a cheetah chasing its prey.
Funny as a clown squeezing into a tiny car.
Kind as friends helping each other when they are hurt.
Happy as someone at a party.
Scary as a haunted house.
Cute as a kitten asleep.

Tay Morey (8)
Crowfoot Community Primary School, Beccles

I Am . . .

Funny as a clown jumping through a hoop of fire.
Friendly as a crocodile not eating a frog.
Cheeky as a monkey dropping a coconut on a zookeeper's head.
Helpful as my mum tidying my bedroom.
Crazy as a dog chasing a cat.
As lively as a bunch of children at a party.

Suzi Robinson (8)
Crowfoot Community Primary School, Beccles

I Am . . .

Fast as a cheetah racing.
Funny as an hilarious joke.
Friendly as a dog licking my face.
Happy as a dog playing with a ball.
Cheeky as a monkey throwing coconuts at the zookeeper.

Stuart Moon (8)
Crowfoot Community Primary School, Beccles

I Am . . .

Funny as a clown falling off a one-wheel bike.
Cheerful as a good friend playing a funny show.
Cheeky as a monkey nicking people's underpants.
Quiet as a little lion sleeping with its mum.
Friendly as friends playing a game of 'it'.
Crazy as a monkey throwing banana skins.

Sarah Playford (8)
Crowfoot Community Primary School, Beccles

I Am...

Cheeky as a monkey throwing coconuts on the zookeeper's head.
Loud as an elephant stomping on a rock.
Fast as a horse galloping in a meadow.
Cool as a penguin wearing sunglasses and a hat.
Pretty as a tulip growing in the sun.
Graceful as a flower swaying in the wind.
Cute as a baby sleeping in a cot.
Impatient as a lion wanting meat.

Millie Anderson (8)
Crowfoot Community Primary School, Beccles

I Am...

Funny as a clown having a pie in the face.
Cheeky as a monkey stealing a doughnut.
Loud as a music band playing.
Fast as a hyena racing against a motorbike.
Helpful as a teacher helping out.
Quiet as a newborn kitten.
Cute as a curled up puppy.
Silly as a cat getting stuck.

Kyesha Gilham (8)
Crowfoot Community Primary School, Beccles

I Am . . .

Funny as a clown throwing water at people.
Fast as a racing car on the track.
Friendly as a dog licking my face.
Cheeky as a monkey throwing bananas at the zookeeper.

Kieran Hart (8)
Crowfoot Community Primary School, Beccles

I Am . . .

Big as a hippo swimming in a pool
Slow as a snail leaving a trail along the path.
Thin as a tall tree.
Little as a mouse that has just been born.
Quiet as a baby kitten.

Kate Alexander (8)
Crowfoot Community Primary School, Beccles

I Am . . .

Funny as a clown squeezing into a car.
Loud as a child screaming like an idiot.
Cool as a cucumber wearing glasses.
Mad as a monkey driving a car.
Fast as a cheetah running.

Isaac Coleman (8)
Crowfoot Community Primary School, Beccles

I Am . . .

Funny as a clown jumping in a swimming pool.
Kind as my mum looking after me.
Speedy as a cheetah catching its prey.
Big as a gorilla smashing at its cage.

Harrison Wright (8)
Crowfoot Community Primary School, Beccles

I Am . . .

Fast as a racing car zooming along
Funny as a clown balancing on a beach ball
Cheeky as a monkey nicking his friend's toy
Graceful as a poppy swaying in the breeze
Patient as a lion waiting to pounce on his prey
Quiet as a mouse waiting for a slice of cheese.

Cerys Russell (8)
Crowfoot Community Primary School, Beccles

I Am . . .

Funny as a clown throwing a pie at another clown.
Cheeky as a monkey throwing coconuts at kids.
Cute as a kitten purring.
Fast as a cheetah chasing its tail.
Strong as a bear climbing a tree.

Callum Homes (8)
Crowfoot Community Primary School, Beccles

Being Afraid

I was afraid to do the monkey bars when I was six.
I was afraid to read a poem to my mum when I was five.
I was afraid to go to a new school.
I was afraid of my cat.

Ellie Giles (7)
Duchy of Lancaster CE Methwold Primary School, Thetford

Limerick

There once was an old woman called Dot
Who liked to sit on a pot
When she sat down
Her trousers fell down
She liked it quite a lot!

Daniel Bailey (10)
Duchy of Lancaster CE Methwold Primary School, Thetford

Haikus

A wrinkled farmer
an old, poor, lonely widow
old Vietnamese

A calm, old lady
standing on a massive hill
looking at the view

Happy, old lady
smiling with sweet happiness
her life had passed by.

Wil Doughty (9)
Duchy of Lancaster CE Methwold Primary School, Thetford

Limerick

There once was a man called Billy
Who was always a little bit silly
He walked to the pier
With gold and beer
And he danced with pretty young Milly.

Ally-Jane Scott Stevenson (10)
Duchy of Lancaster CE Methwold Primary School, Thetford

Limerick

There was once an old man in Spain
Who always got stuck in the rain
So he ate his spaghetti
In a town called Canetti
Some people thought it a pain.

Reuben Cocksedge (10)
Duchy of Lancaster CE Methwold Primary School, Thetford

Haikus

Old, wrinkled lady
smiling with sweet happiness
smiling old lady

The lady is brave
a wonderful explorer
an old explorer

Wonderful grandma
on a mystical journey
poor, lonely widow.

Jazmine Rebecca Murray (10)
Duchy of Lancaster CE Methwold Primary School, Thetford

Limerick

There once was a man with big ears
Who tried to solve his fears
He sat and read
And turned bright red
And all he did was drink beers.

Lewis Bunten (10)
Duchy of Lancaster CE Methwold Primary School, Thetford

Haikus

Brave time traveller
Smiling with much happiness
Peaceful, old lady

Single, old lady
A young boy is on her back
Wonderful lady

Happy, old lady
An old and lonely widow
Wrinkled old lady.

William Kimber (9)
Duchy of Lancaster CE Methwold Primary School, Thetford

Limerick

There was an old lady who was fat
She had a dog and a cat
She went to buy a pie
Wearing a colourful tie
She got back home and saw a rat.

Kia Byrne (9)
Duchy of Lancaster CE Methwold Primary School, Thetford

Limerick

There once was a girl called Lily
She was always a tiny bit silly
To become a clown
She painted on a frown
And put on pants that were frilly.

Evie Chaplin (9)
Duchy of Lancaster CE Methwold Primary School, Thetford

Teeth And Bravery

T winkling teeth in my mouth
E ating lovely, crunchy foods
E ndless munching
T ime for a check up!
H ow does bacteria get in?

T earing teeth always tearing
I 'm so lucky to have teeth
M y teeth are very shiny
E veryone can see my teeth.

Bravery is
Getting on my bike
Opening my mouth at the dentist
Knocking on the headmistress' door
Telling my friends how I feel
Showing my work
Saying no
Knocking on someone's door for Halloween.

Olivia Rodwell (8)
Duchy of Lancaster CE Methwold Primary School, Thetford

My Bike

I was afraid to ride my bike without stabilisers when I was five
And now I do it.
I couldn't do cartwheels when I was four
And now I can do them.

Ana Robertson (7)
Duchy of Lancaster CE Methwold Primary School, Thetford

I Felt Afraid

I felt afraid when I had my stabilisers off my bike
I was four
I was afraid when I moved to a different school
I was six
I was afraid when I fell off my bike.

Raith Bailey (7)
Duchy of Lancaster CE Methwold Primary School, Thetford

My Eye Poem

I love my eyes
because I can see nature,

In the morning
I feel my eyes are shining, shining, shining.

My eyes see parties everywhere.

When I go to the beach
my eyes glare at ice cream.

Abbi Bartrum (8)
Duchy of Lancaster CE Methwold Primary School, Thetford

Being Brave

I felt scared when I went on a kayak.
I was 8.

I felt afraid when I got to the top of a climbing wall.
I was 7.

I felt afraid when a giant house spider was in my bedroom.
I was 6.

I felt afraid when I heard fireworks go off.
I was 5.

I felt afraid when I went round my friends.
I was 4.

Jessica Meehan (8)
Duchy of Lancaster CE Methwold Primary School, Thetford

I Was Afraid

I was afraid about my dog.
I was afraid about a new school.
I was scared to go to the dentist.
I was scared about my stabilisers.

Willow King (7)
Duchy of Lancaster CE Methwold Primary School, Thetford

I Felt Afraid

I felt afraid when the Rottweiler from down the street chased me,
I was seven.
I felt afraid when I went to school for the first time,
I was four.
I felt afraid when I had the chicken pox,
I was three.
I felt afraid waking up in my bedroom after it had been painted,
I was three.

Catherine Louise Parker (8)
Duchy of Lancaster CE Methwold Primary School, Thetford

When I Was Little I Was Brave

When I was a little boy I was afraid to ride my bike
with two wheels.
I was six.

I was brave when I got stung by a bee.

When I was at a fair me and my dad went on a ghost train
I was afraid.
I was seven.

Jaime Ramsay (7)
Duchy of Lancaster CE Methwold Primary School, Thetford

Bravery Is . . .

Telling Mum I broke one of her best bracelets.
Eating something you've never tried before.
Trying not to cry when my pet cat died.
When I had trouble with my work and I needed help.

Jessica Webb (8)
Duchy of Lancaster CE Methwold Primary School, Thetford

When I Was Brave

I had courage when I fell off my bike and I got back on,
I was five.
I had courage when it was my first day at school,
I was four.

Katie Manning (7)
Duchy of Lancaster CE Methwold Primary School, Thetford

Being Afraid

I felt afraid to go on a big train,
when I was six.

I felt afraid to go to a really big roller coaster
when I was seven.

I felt afraid to go on an aeroplane,
when I was seven.

I felt afraid to go on a boat,
when I was seven.

Jamie Vowles (8)
Duchy of Lancaster CE Methwold Primary School, Thetford

My Teeth

T earing bits of food with your teeth
E levating chair of fun at the dentist
E ating an apple, oh no, my wobbly tooth fell out.
T ime to go to the bathroom to brush my teeth.
H elp to get rid of bacteria.

Katherine Woods (9)
Duchy of Lancaster CE Methwold Primary School, Thetford

My Teeth Poem

My teeth shining in the sunlight
Twinkling like a star so bright
I feel like a star in the sky, like a night light.

Caitlin Daisy Jupp (8)
Duchy of Lancaster CE Methwold Primary School, Thetford

Being Brave

I was brave when I stood up to people
I was brave when I spoke to people in crowds
I was brave when I sang in front of people
I was brave when I was ill.

Elizabeth Rose Cocksedge (8)
Duchy of Lancaster CE Methwold Primary School, Thetford

Being Frightened

I feel afraid when I go upstairs on my own.
I felt afraid when I went trick or treating at the USA base.
I felt afraid when I got locked in the bathroom for two hours.
I felt afraid when I went to my cousin's for two nights.
I felt afraid when I went to the riding stable for the first time.

Megan Ann Hamilton (9)
Duchy of Lancaster CE Methwold Primary School, Thetford

My Teeth

T winkling teeth shining
E levating seats and fun at the dentist
E ating crispy food
T earing teeth scare bacteria bugs
H ard, bony teeth.

Bonnie Mary Barber (7)
Duchy of Lancaster CE Methwold Primary School, Thetford

About Myself

I felt afraid when I started school
I was four

I felt afraid when I had my first wobbly tooth
I was five.

I felt afraid when my brother scared me,
I was six.

I was brave to take my stabilisers off my bike,
I was four.

Callum West (9)
Duchy of Lancaster CE Methwold Primary School, Thetford

Eyes Staring

Eyes staring
Doing their job
Staring everywhere
Looking about
It's their job.
They see old people chatting about something.
Eyes see anything you do!

Maddison Skye Bunten (7)
Duchy of Lancaster CE Methwold Primary School, Thetford

Untitled

Eyes are for looking
Eyes are for spooking
Eyes are to cry
Eyes laugh, eyes are to blink.

Brennan Scott Stevenson (7)
Duchy of Lancaster CE Methwold Primary School, Thetford

Haikus

Old, wrinkled lady
Anxious old lady smiling
Happy, old lady

Old lady in shock
She has got lots of gladness
Loves her life and more

Wants to tell stories
Is as sweet as you can be
A loving lady.

Rhiannon Weatherley (9)
Duchy of Lancaster CE Methwold Primary School, Thetford

My Bones

B ones make us move.
O n top of your bones is skin.
N o bones can stretch.
E verybody has bones.
S o what will happen if you didn't have bones?

Imogen Rose Pick (8)
Duchy of Lancaster CE Methwold Primary School, Thetford

My Little Teeth

T he loving smile in my mouth
E ating my delicious food
E lectric chairs in the dentist going up and down
T he time is near to crunch my teeth
H elping to look after teeth, make them shiny and clean
   as the dentist likes.

Jasmine Bunten (8)
Duchy of Lancaster CE Methwold Primary School, Thetford

Bravery Is . . .

Speaking in front of everybody.
Telling Mum I broke my top.
Not to be scared of the dog next door.
Telling Dad I lost my toy.
Moving up a class.

Kaleise Bunten (8)
Duchy of Lancaster CE Methwold Primary School, Thetford

Haikus

Brave, wrinkled grandma
Poor, lonely, weathered widow
Old Vietnamese

Old single lady
Carrying her young grandson
Along stony paths

Happy, old lady
Journey of her life has passed
Very hard worker.

Thomas Harper (11)
Duchy of Lancaster CE Methwold Primary School, Thetford

Haiku

Wrinkled old lady
The journey of life passing
Old Vietnamese

Strolling up a hill
Sightseeing lovely country
Smiling as she went

Poor lonely mother
A marvellous explorer
Wonderful grandma.

Grace Howse (9)
Duchy of Lancaster CE Methwold Primary School, Thetford

Limerick

There once was a boy called Bo
Who did not want to show
His terrible scar
Which was better by far
Than his scary rotten toe!

Harry Butcher (9)
Duchy of Lancaster CE Methwold Primary School, Thetford

Haikus

A single mother
Beautiful and nice mother
A hard worker nan.

An exciting life
Her house is so far away
She's a time traveller.

A wrinkled farmer
She's a brave, wrinkled grandma
A great explorer.

Jenna Ramsey (9)
Duchy of Lancaster CE Methwold Primary School, Thetford

Halloween Poem

Vampires are blood-sucking devils
Spiders make wordy webs
Mummies out of death mask tombs
Witches cackle all night long.

Werewolves howl in their daring graves
Bats are flapping and squeaking in the night
Ghosts go *ooooogh* through the night
Pumpkins come alive in your house.

Beware of the unexpected!

Jasmine Loades (7)
Edward Worlledge Community Junior School, Great Yarmouth

Halloween Poem

Bats flap all night
and have a wonderful flight
all day, all night

Vampires are evil blood-sucking devils
they eat you all up.

Spiders make lots of shiny webs and hide
they stay silent as a mouse.

Wolves howl in their daring graves
they come out at night and scare people
they wake up and scream
'Argh!' Ghosts go, 'Oooooh!'
Halloween, it's so scary.

Chloe Smith (7)
Edward Worlledge Community Junior School, Great Yarmouth

Halloween Poem

On a dark night
Strange things happen
Zombies walk to look for their
Next prey

A ghost is very spooky
A bat is noisy
A mummy is very scary
A monster is creepy

Spiders are dark and hairy
Skeletons rattle their bones
Blood-curdling vampires walk the streets
Pumpkins faces glow in the windows.

Harvey Faraday Drake (7)
Edward Worlledge Community Junior School, Great Yarmouth

Halloween Poem

Bats hang upside down and sleep in the day.
They flap their wings and let out ear-piercing squeaks.

Vampires are blood-sucking monsters with red evil eyes.
They search for their next juicy victim.
Then eat it with their spooky fangs.

Wolves hunt for tasty meat.
They tear and rip at flesh when walking through the night.
They will pounce when you least expect.

Witches cackle when they lock people up.
Warts cover their nose and face.
They fly on their brooms, across the moon.

Tia Williams (7)
Edward Worlledge Community Junior School, Great Yarmouth

A Halloween Poem

Candy, candy everywhere.
Blood-dripping zombies give you a scare!
Blood-sucking vampires, flesh-eating too.
Invisible ghosts will say, 'Boo!'
Ghosts are headless too
Murdering monsters, funny Frankenstein.

Vampires snapping with their fangs, allergic to garlic.
Silly spiders hanging on their webs.
Flappy bats go *squeak, squeak, squeak*.
Crazy kids wearing costumes.
Mummies in their creepy coffins.
Ugly, old witches flying on their brooms.

Bone-filled, lively graveyard.
Daring devils, red, the colour of blood.
Skeletons dancing at a disco.
Werewolves howling at the full moon.
Jack-o-lanterns flickering on the windowsill.
Kids are trick or treating.

Misha Marjoram (7)
Edward Worlledge Community Junior School, Great Yarmouth

Boo!

A cackling, blood-curdling poem.

Jumping, sour sweets in kiddie's bags.
Kids having fun everywhere.
Vampire bats squeaking upside down.

Sneaky devils, red as plumpy tomatoes.
Old, worn-out witches flying over the full moon.

Plump pumpkins round as a blood-dripping head.
Pickety skeletons doing the midnight conga.

Kayley Nash (7)
Edward Worlledge Community Junior School, Great Yarmouth

Halloween Poem

Spooky, scary spiders
Blood-sucking vampires
Witches fly on their broomsticks
Devils look for people to kill

Children trick or treating in the night
Skeletons climb out of their coffins
Coffins creak open
The dead walk through the graveyard

Pumpkins glimmer outside people's houses
Witches' cats scratch everyone
Sweets, sweet, sweets, *lots of sweets*
Be careful they don't rot your teeth

Bats fly in a cave and they bite
You run, run, run and
Scream, scream, scream.

Parys Green (7)
Edward Worlledge Community Junior School, Great Yarmouth

Halloween Poem

Blood-dripping zombies
Vampires with sharp teeth
Headless monsters

Squeaky bats
Pumpkins to keep the vampires out
Mummies in coffins.
Children going trick or treating.

Frankenstein eating brains
Spiderwebs in a dusty corner.
Devil killing anybody who gets in his way.
Watch out!

Ben Brown (8)
Edward Worlledge Community Junior School, Great Yarmouth

Halloween Poem

Ghosts spooky.
Zombies headless.
Vampires blood-dripping.
Mummies scary.
Bats squeaking.
Witches cackling in the night.
Scary devils.
Spooky graveyards.
Pumpkins light the spooky streets.
Children trick or treating.
Children dressed in scary costumes.
Jumping out on people.

Chelsea Glover (7)
Edward Worlledge Community Junior School, Great Yarmouth

Halloween

Witches cackle loudly in the spooky night.
Bats squeak as the night gets darker.
Slimy graveyards with floating ghosts.
Orangey pumpkins with candles lighting it.

Mummies wrapped in mouldy bandages.
Blood-sucking vampires in the cold night.
Sweets, sweets, sweets in overflowing bags.
Black spiders camouflaging in the night.

Blood-curling zombies dripping with blood.
Children dressed in spooky and scary outfits.
Devils as red as a red apple.
People trick or treating in the cold, dark night.

Bethany Coulson (7)
Edward Worlledge Community Junior School, Great Yarmouth

Halloween

Scary monsters in the dark.
Pumpkins plump and orange.
Wolves howling in the night.
Witches fly over the moon.
Zombies climb out of graveyards.
Trick or treaters collecting lovely sweets.
I love Halloween.

Dylan Ward (7)
Edward Worlledge Community Junior School, Great Yarmouth

Black And White

Black looks like a dull and deep night.
White looks like an angelic day full of happiness.
Black sounds like ear-piercing fear all over.
White sounds like a gentle and calm river.
Black smells like burnt toast in an ancient toaster.
White smells like a brand new piece of crisp white paper.
Black tastes like a bitter and sour lemon.
White tastes like fresh and pure mountain water.
Black feels like a rough leather jacket.
White feels like a piece of smooth silk.

Shenel Mushtaq (10)
Gearies Junior School, Ilford

My Teacher Miss Wyatt

My teacher's name is Miss Wyatt.
She does not need to diet.
She is very funny.
She is like Bugs Bunny.
But she always keeps us quiet.

My teacher she is new.
She knows just what to do.
We always find
She is very kind.
She is very pretty too.

Harriet Smith (8)
Hadleigh Junior School, Benfleet

Underneath The Crooked Floorboards

Underneath the crooked floorboards
What did I find?
A little door right,
Here's a list of what I saw . . .

A mouse trying to pounce
A cat sitting on a tap
A dog eating cod
A pencil using utensils
A map sitting on a lap
A sock watching a clock

Next time you're really bored
Look underneath your crooked floorboards
What you'll find is all a mystery
But I know you'll find a bit of history.

Summer Hall (11)
Hadleigh Junior School, Benfleet

Fireworks Poem

Fireworks, fireworks
We *all* like big fireworks
Bright and colourful or maybe plain
Go and take a photo and put it in a frame
Soup and hot dogs are what you eat
On firework's night for a special treat
Tuck your pets up snuggly and tight
So they don't struggle or get a fright
So remember, remember
That the 5th of November
Is firework's night!

Benjamin Foreman (8)
Hardwick Primary School, Bury St Edmunds

The Pony

The pony is wearing a white silver coat

The pony has sparkling hooves
Clean as glass

The pony has brown and white hair
The pony is a girl called Belle.

Olivia Lingwood (8)
Hardwick Primary School, Bury St Edmunds

Christmas

Christmas is cheerful
Bright and cheeky
You never know what
Will happen next

It's time to cheer
Because Christmas
Is here

Hip hip hooray
Come on let's play

Jump on your sledges everyone
Because Christmas is here
Just have some fun

Christmas is a secret
Don't you see?
It's trying to trick us
So be as quiet as a flea

Christmas, Christmas.

Chloe Sparks (8)
Hardwick Primary School, Bury St Edmunds

My Fat Cat

Midge is my cat
he's very fat
he eats fish
from a dish
black and hairy
soft and spotty
he has sharp claws
he has scratched the doors!

Chanel Healy (8)
Hartest CE VC Primary School, Bury St Edmunds

Zoom, Zoom, Zoom

Zoom, zoom, zoom,
I'm going to the moon,
Zoom, zoom, zoom,
I will get there soon,
If you want to take a trip
Climb aboard in my rocket ship,
Zoom, zoom, zoom,
I'm going to the moon.

Zara Smith (8)
Hartest CE VC Primary School, Bury St Edmunds

The Moon

The moon is a bright silver Christmas bauble
that drifts through space.
The moon is glittering tinsel wrapped around a ball.
The moon is white tasty cheese on a pretty round plate.

Michael Oxby (9)
Heycroft Primary School, Leigh-On-Sea

The Stars

The stars are brighter than stadium flood light
if Spain vs. Germany were playing.

They catch your eye while you are walking past the
jewellery shop window.

The stars shoot across the sky like a bonfire
exploding in the air.

They are so sparkly they make your eyes all fuzzy and weird
if you were looking at the sun.

They are like shining stones being thrown up in the atmosphere.

Tigi Whitehouse (9)
Heycroft Primary School, Leigh-On-Sea

Saturn

Saturn is a dusty tornado blowing through clouds
It is a sparkling diamond from a jewellery shop
It is a yellow pepper getting squashed
It is a lemon sitting in a round fruit bowl
It is a sizzling boiling pan going into fire.

Summer Hurley (9)
Heycroft Primary School, Leigh-On-Sea

The Stars

The stars twinkle and sparkle like jewels in a posh jewellery shop.
They are white, sizzling, sparklers held by little excited children
on firework night.
They are white polished twinkly earrings worn by the teacher.
They shine like crystals ready to be dug up from the ground.
The stars shine like money in a hidden treasure box in a cave.

Kloe Snowdon (9)
Heycroft Primary School, Leigh-On-Sea

The Planets

Jupiter is a giant volcano exploding like lightning and attacking the surface of the ground.

Mercury is a dark, grey pavement on a wet morning.

The sun is a burning flame coming down from a firework.

Daniel Seaman (9)
Heycroft Primary School, Leigh-On-Sea

The Sun

The sun is like a shiny piece of foil thrown into the gloomy bin.
It is a bright bonfire on green grass.
It is a light bulb hanging from the ceiling.
It is a yellow ball bouncing on the ground.
It is a star up in the sky shining down on me.

Morgan Woodward (9)
Heycroft Primary School, Leigh-On-Sea

Gigantic Jupiter

Jupiter's colours are like slithery snakes
of orange, brown and cream on a wet branch.

It is an orange ball bouncing rapidly in the freezing playground.

It is a juicy orange lying on the window sill.

It is a volcano wasteland burning out lava every second.

Luke Collins (9)
Heycroft Primary School, Leigh-On-Sea

The Sun

It is a big ball of fire from a dragon's mouth
with sparks shooting out angrily.

It is a shining gold coin in a treasure chest in a deep dark cave.

It is a ruby and amber burning while littering in the sky.

It is a yellow car headlight shining in the night.

Mason Wakeling (10)
Heycroft Primary School, Leigh-On-Sea

Pluto

Pluto is the hairy brown skin of a kiwi.
It is a smooth brown conker on a massive black tree.
It is a sticky chocolate bar in a sparkling wrapper.
It is a dark brown ball in a shallow, dark bag.
It is dark like dirty trousers covered in mud.
It is light brown like a light brown egg.

Emma Partner (9)
Heycroft Primary School, Leigh-On-Sea

Fortunate Earth

The Earth is emerald, blue seaweed floating in the ocean!
It is a blue seed on a green round leaf!
It is a splash of blue and green paint in my black art book!
It is a glowing torch of light shining in the darkness.
It is a dry, arid ball of clay on a school art room.

Isobel Dowden (10)
Heycroft Primary School, Leigh-On-Sea

Stars

The stars are shining pearls that lay deep down the in ocean.
They are golden coins in a treasure chest
They are fairies on a Christmas tree
They are thousands of rubies twinkling in a cave
They are wax candle lights burning down
They are millions of diamonds in a jewellery shop.

Ellise Pratt (9)
Heycroft Primary School, Leigh-On-Sea

The Planets

The moon it is an Aston Martin going to a party.
Uranus is a blue ball going down an empty street.
The sun is an amber crystal thrown into a fire.
Mars is a lightsaber going to zap someone.
Saturn is an amber diamond in a ruined temple.

Will Fenton (9)
Heycroft Primary School, Leigh-On-Sea

Glimmering Stars

The stars are a bright white twinkling fountain in the blue night sky
They are stunning glimmering rocks about 2000m tall
They are white diamonds in a boutique shop
They are a cool Nokia phone with a sparkly silver case
It is a white puff of smoke spraying from a spray can.

Jessica Hawes (9)
Heycroft Primary School, Leigh-On-Sea

The Stars

The stars are diamonds twinkling in a window of an antique shop.
They are bits of fairy dust sparkling on a fairy's wand.
They are tiny little specks of pollen from a flower.
They are tiny balls of fire thrown into space
by a juggler from a circus.
They are tiny sparks from sparklers on Bonfire Night.

Star Bewley (9)
Heycroft Primary School, Leigh-On-Sea

Stars

The stars are like gleaming pearls at the bottom of the sparkly sea.

They are eye catching diamonds sitting
in a dark jewellery shop window.

They are sparkling stones lying on the sunny seaside.

They are balls of flames sizzling in a hot oven.

They are shiny blades of glass being thrown up high in the sky.

Chloe Nall (10)
Heycroft Primary School, Leigh-On-Sea

The Sun

The sun is a giant burning powerhouse burning day and night.
It is an amber football thrown into a dark stadium.
It is an orange amber jewel burning into the flames.
It is a pure heatwave burning everything in its path.
It is a storm of air heating the sky.
It is a radiator in a dark lounge heating everything.

Joe Haines (9)
Heycroft Primary School, Leigh-On-Sea

Mars

Mars is a massive, red apple that lies in a dark, black fruit bowl.
It is a splodge of red, slushy paint stuck in my raven black art book.
It is a bumpy red jewel ready to be cracked out of a rock.
It is a dusty, red globe spinning rapidly in an old, cobwebbed geography class.
It is scarlet lava from a gigantic erupting volcano.

Creág MacDonald (10)
Heycroft Primary School, Leigh-On-Sea

Sun

The sun is a burning hot bonfire on the 5th of November.
It is a red, ripe apple sitting on the window sill.
It is a knobbly brown twig that has been burnt by a camp fire.

Dean Morriss (9)
Heycroft Primary School, Leigh-On-Sea

The Sun

The sun is a huge explosion on a battlefield.
It is a scorching yellow ball sitting happily in a pitch-black garden.
It is a great fireball being launched from a huge catapult.
It's a bright car light on a frosty dark night.

Ryan Brooks (9)
Heycroft Primary School, Leigh-On-Sea

Pluto

Pluto is a burnt brown ant with cracks shaped like lightning.
It is a rock rolling behind all the other planets away from the sun.
It is a spot of brown paint on a black piece of paper.
It is a boy's mini brown football kicked into the sky.
It is a bumpy piece of bubble wrap dropped on the floor.

Christopher Ho (9)
Heycroft Primary School, Leigh-On-Sea

Burning Sun

The sun is a ruby and amber crystal shining in the sky.
It is a burning bomb waiting to explode!
It is a fiery, sizzling and burning volcano waiting to erupt.

Thomas Barnard (9)
Heycroft Primary School, Leigh-On-Sea

Planet Pluto

Planet Pluto is an elephant's eye up high in the black, dark space
It is a colourful, sparkling marble dangling up above.
It is a tiny, shiny white saucer.
It s a freezing, little emerald green tennis ball.

Darcie Catling (9)
Heycroft Primary School, Leigh-On-Sea

Venus

Venus is a sparkly turquoise lollipop,
It is a huge, turquoise lollipop spinning
It is a hula hoop that is very close to the sun,
It is a glittery disco ball spinning fast in the sky.

Maisie Spicer (9)
Heycroft Primary School, Leigh-On-Sea

Space

The sun is a burning puddle that slowly crawls behind me.
It is a glowing football that slowly crawls behind me.
It is a melting piece of chocolate which sticks me to the ground.
It is a crackling grasshopper which makes my ears burn.
Pluto is a freezing marble that makes me shiver.
It is a frozen fridge that makes me hungry.
It is a frozen iceberg which makes me trip over.
It is a shivering dinosaur that freezes me.
Jupiter is a huge bowling ball which is impossible to throw.
It is a mind-blowing hurricane that throws me miles away.
It is a massive galaxy which makes the Saturn rocket turn into an ant.
It is a destructive tree that attacks everything.

Oliver Towning (10)
Heycroft Primary School, Leigh-On-Sea

The Sun

The sun is a gigantic Pacman glowing in the sky.

Saturn is a massive yellow ball stuck in the sky
between two black holes.

Jumping Jupiter is so massive, taller than the Eiffel Tower.

Joseph Barnard (9)
Heycroft Primary School, Leigh-On-Sea

The Sun

The sun is a sparkly disco ball shining across the universe.
It is a fiery hot oven with sharp burning pins.
It is watching every planet go past him every day.
It is not scared of anything at all.

Tom Cracknell (10)
Heycroft Primary School, Leigh-On-Sea

Saturn Is . . .

Saturn is a beautiful ice rink with ice so thin it shines with the sun's bright reflection.

It is a massive gassy pub that smells like freshly cooked BBQ.

It is a deadly confused rhino ready to run and pull you in and crush you into a million tiny strips of flesh.

It is a breaking disco ball that has been smashed into pieces in a dark pit of never-ending space.

It is a snow tiger, cute and fluffy on the outside,
but really fierce inside.

Thomas Gavriel (10)
Heycroft Primary School, Leigh-On-Sea

Saturn

Saturn is a large glowing igloo of frozen ice.
It is a freezing cold ice statue of people.
It is a puff of smoke made from ice.
It is an ice army of minions for an ice sculptor.

Michael Jones (9)
Heycroft Primary School, Leigh-On-Sea

Galaxy

A galaxy is a plate of glitter swirling and twisting in the sky
It is a huge blast of dust sparkling constantly
It is a mass of green, blue, yellow and red sequins scattered across a sheet of black paper
It is an endless sea of dust and glitter in space
It is a desert of stars.

William Abbott (9)
Heycroft Primary School, Leigh-On-Sea

The Stars

The stars are silvery sparkles of glitter that shine
in the pitch-black blanket of the sky.

It is a non-stop glow of beauty that dances
in the plain horizon of space.

It is forever flashing elegantly; like torch lights in a dark cave.

It is a twinkling diamond like sequins and gold.

It is a sprinkling light of sapphire and emerald prettiness.

Freya Morton (9)
Heycroft Primary School, Leigh-On-Sea

Venus Is . . .

Venus is a big lumpy, bumpy chocolate ball
with hints of vanilla in the dust desert of Egypt.
It is a laser beam of shining sapphire and glowing topaz.
It's a swaying cloud in the dark night sky.

Alice Martin (9)
Heycroft Primary School, Leigh-On-Sea

Venus Is . . .

Venus is a deadly scorching hot beach
that no one would want to go on
It is a massive heat bomb exploding its volcanic gas in the night sky
It is a death zone that snatches and keeps anything that enters it
It is a killer that will try to catch more and more heat
by the second.

Alice Wise
Heycroft Primary School, Leigh-On-Sea

Uranus

Uranus is a swirling green and blue lollipop of burning gas and bubbling boiling water

It is a Wampa from Star Wars eating animals in space.

Alfie Taylor (9)
Heycroft Primary School, Leigh-On-Sea

Sun And Stars

The sun
The sun is like an angry oven steaming back at you.
It is a pizza sizzling with huge speckles of cheese,
It is a pool of boiling red water.
It is a calm ocean of orange, red and white settling in the night sky.

The stars
Stars are white glowing apples.
They are like millions of tiny disco balls glistening like silver baubles.
They are thousands of diamonds just laying there in the sky carelessly without any thought.
They are wrapped in a gold blanket with a background of jet-black carbon paper.

Katie Bourdillon (9)
Heycroft Primary School, Leigh-On-Sea

My Mum

I really love my mum.
She supports me in everything I do.
She is kind and generous.
Her smile can brighten any moment.
Her hugs lift my spirit.
I never have to worry when she's nearby.
She tells me off when I'm naughty.
She wants me to behave properly.
She fills my heart with gladness.
She is the best mum in the world.

Jack Christie (10)
Hurst Primary School, Bexley

Playtime

As the children come out to play
The playground turns to clay
Some children play ball
And the playground is cool
Some children chat
But the playground doesn't like that
The whistle is blown
The playground is alone.

Tom Shea (10)
Hurst Primary School, Bexley

Popcorn

I see it popping in the machine
I love the noise it makes
Sweet or salt or with some butter
It really tastes so great
In the cinema or at home
It doesn't matter to me
I know that if I had to choose
I'd eat it for my tea!

Ezrie Cornford (10)
Hurst Primary School, Bexley

Hobbies

Karate, kicking and punching, hard and soft,
Self-defence and fitness training with my friends

Kenjutsu graceful and dangerous working with a sword,
Slow and fast, building trust with your friends.

Guitar, notes build slowly sounding rough and scratchy,
Practise more and more to create a song to make my friends smile.

Football, I play after school in the park, fast and hard,
Running and scoring goals with my friends to win a match.

Harry Powley (10)
Hurst Primary School, Bexley

Football

We talk about the ref making bad decisions
Celebrating as your team wins, jumping around and screaming
Showing off to your friends because you got the new kit
Saying to your friends, look who's at the top of the league
Happy 'cause you got the game on a console
Getting upset because your team lost to an easy team
Screaming your head when your team score
Being at a live match and being on TV.

Kyle Anthony David Brown (10)
Hurst Primary School, Bexley

Cooking Time

Pancakes, meatballs, pizza, chips
Flip, cook, fry and make
This is what I like to bake
But most of all it's chocolate cake.

Measure, stir, mix and drizzle
Cook the sausages: *sizzle, sizzle.*
Add the spice, herbs and flavour
Creating dishes for all to savour.

Cooking meals is so much fun
Inventing recipes for everyone.

Tegan Battersby (10)
Hurst Primary School, Bexley

Peace

The colour of peace is turquoise
Peace sounds like the turning of a page in a book
Peace smells like a clean fabric sofa
Peace is a picture of someone sound asleep
Peace feels as if you are in a completely different world
to everyone
Peace reminds me of a hot summer's day,
listening to the waves crash against the shore.

Emily Jenson (10)
Hurst Primary School, Bexley

Love

Love is yummy chocolate melting in my mouth.
Love is like a never-ending kiss that goes on and on.
Love is a warm, fluffy teddy bear holding on to me.
Love is blossom falling slowly like a beating heart.
Love is like a cute baby, warm and cuddly.
Love is a really warm dressing gown, soft and huggable.

Ellie Owen (10)
Hurst Primary School, Bexley

Loss

Loss makes us feel unhappy
Loss makes us feel sad
Loss can make us remember the love
Loss makes me miss my dog, Barney.

Joe Williams (10)
Hurst Primary School, Bexley

Barney - My Friend

Barney was a very special dog
he had silky russet fur
he was always a happy dog
waggly tail and cold coal-black nose
he always used to come and sit with me
and he was playful and protected me
he loved his chocolate
and I loved him.

Isabella Kane (10)
Hurst Primary School, Bexley

Smelly Feet

My sister's feet are slimline and neat.
Her toenails are bright red, she paints them in her big, big bed.
She massages scented cream into her feet
And leaves an unusual perfume on the sheet.
I have set the scene of these manicured feet
But boy oh boy, do my sister's feet reek!

Eliane Newitt (10)
Hurst Primary School, Bexley

The Princess And Bob

There once was a princess
With a pink dress
She lived in a castle with a moat and the only way across was by boat
She was in love with Sir Bob
Who hadn't got a job.
He slept all day, and got no pay
He was really just a slob.
The king and queen had had enough,
With a huff and a puff they sent Bob packing with all his stuff.

Jamie Mitchell (10)
Hurst Primary School, Bexley

Fairy Tales

Fairy stories are full of tales,
Like wicked witches, toads and snails.
To princes and princesses who fall in love,
To scaly dragons who breathe fire from above.
Also those little pigs running with fear,
As the evil wolf gets near.
Has it not had enough of old Granny?
Does he really need to eat the little hammies?
Then there is Jack who sold his cow
And the five magic beans which made everyone go wow!
We can't forget fairies, who are full of magic,
Some can be real kind but some can be tragic
And the little ugly duckling who turned into a swan,
To princesses who end up marrying a frog.
Bedtime stories are full of adventure,
Some are scary, some are fun
But what would we do and be without one?

Paige Bridger (10)
Hurst Primary School, Bexley

My Dog!

My dog is big
My dog is strong
Her eyes are bright
Her fur is long.

My dog is big
My dog is funny
She loves it when
I tickle her tummy.

My dog is big
My dog is great
I love my dog
She is like my mate.

Lewis Watson (11)
Hurst Primary School, Bexley

Once Upon A Time

Once upon a time
There was a greedy bear,
He had lots of hair.
He lived in the forest which was dark green and horrid
And on one dark and dismal day
That greedy bear went out to play.

He wandered round the children's park
It was almost getting dark.
Looking for which one to eat
He chose the one with the largest feet.
Big and round, tall from the ground,
That's the one he growled around.

'No, no, no,' there came a shriek
'Away from him, he's rather weak.
How dare you choose my son to eat
No go away and take this sweet.'

Off he trumbled,
Grizzly, just mumbled.
Back to his den,
Where he ate a hen.

Harrison Callard (10)
Hurst Primary School, Bexley

Fruit!

Apples, bananas, oranges and plums
You don't need a spoon just use your fingers and your thumbs
It's easy and quick, you can eat it on the run
So you don't have to stop when you're having lots of fun.
Make sure you get all your fill five-a-day,
You don't have to stop, you can eat it on the way.
It's full of goodness and really, really sweet,
You can put it in the juicer, it tastes really, really neat.
So when you want a snack, give the sweets the boot
And always make sure you eat lots and lots of fruit.

Jamie Lyons (10)
Hurst Primary School, Bexley

The Young Dragon

'What can I do?' Young Dragon cried,
'I've huffed and puffed, I sure have tried.
It doesn't matter how hard I blow
My fire will not glow.

My scales are cold, I must be ill.'
'You can't be a dragon,' Mother cried.
'Let's take you to the doctor, he will know
Why your throat is so dry.'

The doctor came and looked and said,
'You may need to go to bed.
Just drink this petrol and eat these screws,
They will warm your body through.'

'I drank the petrol and ate the screws
My tummy burbled and began to light.
As fiery sparks flew out my mouth,
I stood there in delight.'

Brooke Connell (10)
Hurst Primary School, Bexley

Sea

The sea is sparkling in the moonlight
The sea is deep with colourful fish
They swim all day and night
When crabs pinch it hurts a lot
So be careful if they do
Otherwise you might be human stew!

Savannah Golesworthy (10)
Hurst Primary School, Bexley

Goal!

The whistle blows to start the game
I hope we have fun again.

I play with number seven on my back
We move around the pitch in a pack.

The ball gets passed to number ten
He goes past two or three men.

He whips in a cross
I'm waiting in the right spot.

An overhead kick, I think to myself
The keeper stands there without any help.

'Goal!' is screamed from all the fans
The loudest scream is from my old man.

The match is won
And we're on top
Hope we stay there and beat the lot.

Goal!

Joseph Hopper (11)
Hurst Primary School, Bexley

Moonlight

M e, I am a bright twinkling planet in the darkness to come.
O odles of light shines down from me.
O h, the light on the water below.
N ight-time is the time for me.
L et's light up the darkness now the time is right.
I light up the sky like a magical firefly.
G olden glow, warm and soft.
H ot, I'm not just big and bright.
T ime passes by - the morning appears, tonight I will be back.

Emily Roffey (10)
Hurst Primary School, Bexley

Hats

Mop hats, top hats,
Shiny hats, tiny hats,
Lacy hats, spacey hats,
Hard hats, guard hats,
Hat with strings,
Hats with wings,
Hats with feathers
And hats for all weathers,
Hats with flowers,
And hats you could look at for hours and hours.

Lauren Couldwell (10)
Hurst Primary School, Bexley

A Princess's Dream

Princess Mary was her name
Anything that went wrong she was to blame
Under tables she tied people's shoes in knots
She painted her palace pink with purple dots
The girl was outrageous and ugly
But one night when she was in her bed all snuggly
Prince Charming rode by, climbed the palace way up high
Princess Mary awoke from bed, Charming said with a sigh
'You're not ugly at all,' and belovedly kissed her
And they lived happily ever after.

Ellie Lenzi (10)
Hurst Primary School, Bexley

Daydream

It is a daydream like I have never had before, it is wonderful
I am in Paris seeing the sunny side of things, it is beautiful;

I take a sniff of the red rose flower
Underneath the Eiffel Tower;

I take a look through the shop window where I see
a great bundle of French cheese
Then I think, *shall I go and have a look at Monet's art
in the gallery?*

I smell the gorgeous scent of food
And wander into the Le Grand Véfour where I develop
a very good mood;

I come to a shop named Coco Chanel
And try on a beautiful blue and white beret;

I take a trip down to a marvellous beach called Saint-Jean-de-Luz
I cannot wait to tell all my friends and family
they are going to be so jealous;

I get taken back to reality when I hear a loud boom
It is coming from the clouds above, making a shudder of thunder that filled
the whole room.

Megan Sweeney (10)
Hurst Primary School, Bexley

Is Someone In Your Family Magical?

Well there's a magical person in mine,
She has purple eyes and green hair, but looks very fine!
She dances all day, sings all night
And isn't afraid to have a fight.
She trips over herself all the time,
Barely knows how to rhyme.
Her feet smell like cheese
And she never ever says please.
She picks her nose,
Has lots of foes.
She doesn't wash,
Obviously isn't posh.
Has long nails,
Always eating snails.
Very vain,
Definitely insane.
She has a wart on the left side of her ugly face,
With cats and mice she enjoys to play chase.
Every day she wears a long black dress
And dreams she is a beautiful princess.
She eats all day
And gets tooth decay.
As she eats all the sweets,
No fruits or beets.
She jumps on her broomstick, and up to her room,
Lies in her bed, her bed of doom.
What on Earth is she doing now?
She is probably doing something evil, but how?
There's someone magical in my family.
Is there someone magical in yours?

Melisa Chakarto (10)
Hurst Primary School, Bexley

My Pet Dog

My pet dog is grey
And she likes to play.
Her name is Piper
And she is very hyper.
When she is at the park
She likes to bark.
She likes to bite
Or chase a kite.
She likes to have a pat
But is scared of a cat.
She likes to have a sniff
But gives us a bad whiff.
She has long legs
And likes to chew pegs.
When she is asleep
No one dares to take a peep.

Maddie Wheale (10)
Hurst Primary School, Bexley

My Brother

My brother is so mean
He's an idiotic machine.
He always wants me to cry
I just don't know why.
He wrestles with my dad
Till he gets mad.
He always crosses the line
Every single time.
We have to share a room
It's like a human tomb.
But he's still my brother
Because we have the same mother.
He's always there for me
I'm very glad he's on my family tree.
Even when I'm in trouble and I take the blame
He is my brother and it will stay the same.

Adam De Bolla (10)
Hurst Primary School, Bexley

Wizard And Witch

Wizard was a young man
His name was Dan.
Witch was a young lady
Her name was Sadie.
The wizard zapped up a massive ramp
To forget about his awful cramp.
The witch made a potion
And disguised it like a bottle of lotion.
Witch hated Wizard
She thought he was an evil lizard.
Wizard hated Witch
He thought she was evil and slick.
They fought all the time
They even blamed each other for their own crimes.
Rabbit was getting a pain from this
Next he was going to make sure they missed.
So he picked up a big piece of driftwood
And held it high in the middle of both houses and stood.
Witch tossed an enchanted axe at Wizard's house
Wizard did the same while chasing a mouse.
Both enchanted axes landed on either side of the driftwood
Then Rabbit placed the driftwood on the floor as gently as he could.
Both Wizard and Witch stepped outside holding cups
And greeted each other and made up.
After that they never gave me a pain
And they never fought with each other again.

Aqil Sabir (10)
Hurst Primary School, Bexley

My Unusual Sister

My sister has
Long blonde hair
Big blue eyes
And skin so fair

When night-time comes
You should see
She doesn't look
Like you or me

Her lovely eyes
Turn black and scary
Her nails curl up
And her hands get hairy

Her back hunches over
Her skin turns green
Spots and warts appear
The worst you've ever seen

When darkness fades
And morning has come
She's back to herself
The beautiful one.

Ellie Badcock (11)
Hurst Primary School, Bexley

Spectacular School

At the start of school we have our register
Which is taken by our teacher Mr Lesiter.
A, B, C is what we do next in the day
We learn different subjects in every different way.
Next is our half an hour break
When I have my fruit but not my cake.
Maths is after, we do 1, 2, 3
Next comes singing, we do 'Doe Ray Me'.
Lunch is my favourite as we get an hour away
And when we've finished we go back out and play.
After that is science
We're studying the truth about giants.
Joined to that is detective work
Trying to find out what makes things jerk.
At afternoon break
We sit by the lake.
Assembly's in the halls
When we recite all the rules.
Lastly is sport
We play it and try not to get caught.
Finally home time comes our way
But I wonder what they do in an alien's day.

Georgina Doig (11)
Hurst Primary School, Bexley

Once In My Bubble Bath

Once I'm in my bubble bath
I like to stir up more.
Half the suds go in my eyes
And half go on the floor.

The fun is in the bubbles 'cause
They giggle on my skin,
And when I stick them on my face
They dangle from my chin.

When I splash them hard enough
They pop and disappear,
And then my bath time's over 'cause
I've made the water clear.

Casey Jones (10)
Hurst Primary School, Bexley

Cinderella And The Ugly Sister Take The 11 Plus

The ugly sister took the 11 plus
She came in and said she would pass
Cinderella came in without a fuss
She took the test nice and calm
With her pencil firmly in her palm
She went out nice and happy
The sister switched her test with Cinderella's
Three weeks later they had the results
The sister took a little peek
She ripped up the results in disbelief
Cinderella looked at the pieces
Then cheered out with all her might
Proud, happy because she had passed
While the sister was sad and unhappy
Because she did not pass
Seven years later she was in distress
In a complete mess
While Cinderella had success
Maybe it would not have happened if the
Sister had not cheated!

Tendai Joshua Spicer (11)
Hurst Primary School, Bexley

Ugly, Old Witch

Once upon a time there lived an ugly old witch,
She unfortunately lived by a ditch.
Her face was green and had a big red lump
And she smelled rather like a rubbish dump.

She went trick or treating on Halloween night,
Everyone in the neighbourhood got a terrible fright.
'Why are people acting so strange?
I'm acting normal for a change.'

She went back to her house with her hat full of tears
And shook it off with TV and magic beers.
She felt very hungry so she had soup from a tin
And while doing this, she threw her witch's outfit in the bin.

'Next year I will give it another go!'
'Perhaps dressing up, where nobody knows,
That in fact, I am the ugly old witch, who lives by a ditch!'

Fintan Murphy (10)
Hurst Primary School, Bexley

The Robin

When winter comes and snow starts to fall
The robin comes hopping,
Hopping, hopping.
The robin comes hopping and he starts to call,
'Where are my friends,
My friends, my friends?
Where is the snowman and his huge hat?
Where are the snowballs that soar so high?
And where is the fluffy, ginger cat?'
So off he flew, searching in vain for his friends.

Miranda Parkin (10)
Hurst Primary School, Bexley

Jack And The Beanstalk

There once was a family that was very, very rich
They had their own private football pitch
The family had a nasty child
Who really was extremely wild

His name was Jack and he was thirteen years old
He was very greedy, he was often told
Jack once saw his mother's jewels
And he decided to break the rules

He went to market and met a man called Dean
Who was willing to trade Jack's jewels for a magic bean
Jack swapped his goods and ran straight to his field
Where he planted the beans and then chilled

Jack waited and waited for his beans to sprout
And when it reached the sky, he wondered what it was all about
He climbed the plant right to the top
Where he met a troll with hair like a mop

Jack stared at the troll and then thumped him on the back
He ran into the troll's castle; oh that silly Jack.
There was gold everywhere; Jack looked around in a daze
He was so happy that his eyes sparkled like the sun's rays

Jack had found his most happy place
He snatched everything like it was a race
Ran out of the castle and down the beanstalk
He bumped into his mum and excitedly started to talk

He opened his pockets but the gold was gone
The magic bean was back and it hardly shone
'That'll teach you a lesson, you greedy boy,' the troll mocked
Jack looked up at the troll completely and utterly shocked

After that day Jack was never greedy again
And all the good people said, 'Amen!'

Suzanna Page (11)
Hurst Primary School, Bexley

Cinnella White In Wonderland

Cinnella White works in the cellar, she had no friends, only Bella.
Who was very much at least, married to a beast, but hated if you would tell her.
Cinnella slept on a pea, when she realised, she went to see,
Cinnella can't touch water, if she does she'll be King Triton's daughter!
Triton is the king of all the seas.
He has the torso of the man, but a large fish tail instead of his knees.
He beholds a trident in his hands,
So he could frighten the villains in the underwater lands
Cinnella can also sleep for 100 years
Without making a peep, no fears or no tears!
She waits for her handsome prince, who missed her ever since
To give her that one kiss!
She waits for him in her tower, he should come in about an hour!
She's got long blonde hair, so long that you can't help but stare.
Her prince climbs up her gold locks to be with her forever,
And not waste time on the clocks.
When she walks on the road, she falls down a deep black hole
Into a mysterious place by the name Wonderland!
Wonderland is a place where there's magic
But not tragic, except the queen, the evil queen,
The Queen of Hearts, that is very mean!
Cinnella grew big, Cinnella grew small, that wasn't weird at all!
She had seven little helpers who were dwarfs and are truly small but
Like to dig for gold
There's . . . Sneezy, Sleepy, Dopey, Doc, Happy, Bashful and Grumpy!
She had a witch of a stepmother who thought she was the best
Until she chanted at the mirror one day and said, 'Mirror, mirror on the wall, who's the fairest of them all?'
But the mirror replied, 'Cinnella White.'
'What?' she yelled in a fright, she had a plan, but it got ban
Cinnella White lived happily ever after with her man!

Ahmed Negm (11)
Hurst Primary School, Bexley

Harvest Poem

We are so lucky
But the poor aren't
Remember to give
And remember to share

We are so lucky for what we have
So why don't we think of those that don't
Compare us two
We are so rich

You would be amazed
At the place children are raised
In one chair and dirty water
Then look at what we've got
Nice warm beds and fresh water

Safe house to be warm
And feel really safe too
Why do the poor need to roam
To find a place to sleep?

We have medical
Whenever we are ill
Those who don't
Die
With tears running down the faces
Of that child's family

So let's be grateful
For what we have
So let's pray to God
And hope He sends the message.

Charlotte Ing (11)
Kingston Primary School, Benfleet

War Poem

Here we go again, the bombs, the blood and the deaths,
why does this happen every year?
One day the target will hit right here.

So I sit here every day praying,
'Lord please don't let me die today.'
I am so scared to go out there, even to go to the bunkers to share.

But I don't care, if I die I want to die in peace
even though my wife didn't.
One day I will meet her up in Heaven
laying on a fluffy cloud like a feather.
This is why I hate war
And this is why I hate war.

David Batchelor (10)
Kingston Primary School, Benfleet

I Thought . . .

A long time ago my good lad
Wilson was with me.
Then the little paper boy said, 'A war is out,'
Then one morning my mum said,
'It's time for you to go out fighting.'
So I went to a river in Belgium
It was called the Somme
Then me and Wilson stayed as close as possible
Then the worse words of my life came from Sergeant Jimmy
He said, 'We are attacking the enemy trenches tonight,'
So at 12 o'clock we faced all those machine guns
And my good lad Wilson was never seen again
They said it was the last Great War
I thought it was the last Great War
I thought wrong.

Thomas Elliott (10)
Kingston Primary School, Benfleet

Why War?

I'm sitting here in 1944,
With my gas mask, feeling poor,
I am a man who awaits his end,

Newspapers and rationing,
Bombs crashing, over and over again,
Pictures on the wall of my wife and me,
Praying to the Lord that she will forgive me,

Time goes by and I will be dead soon,
Please don't leave me,
You will be with me soon,
You will be with me soon.

Lavinia Tidy-Jones (10)
Kingston Primary School, Benfleet

Thankful Poem

The food on your plate,
the farmer works hard
to get food for you and me that we take for granted.

The farmer in his JCB and his digger
working hard to get the food to you,
all the peas, carrots, beans and milk came from a farm.

Think how lucky you are to have food,
some people don't!
Thank you to farmers for the food you bring to us.

James Hill (10)
Kingston Primary School, Benfleet

Save The Forest!

As brown, crunchy leaves
tumble from the sky
The trees sway and creak
and a tear comes to my eye.
How could they destroy
this brilliant place of merry and joy?
How could they just kill
all the animals and their homes?
Do they do it for a thrill
or do they feel it in their bones?

The sound of tweeting birds
is one of the most beautiful sounds.
The deer travel in their herds
attracting many crowds.
I don't understand why they have to destroy this place!
I don't understand why they have to destroy this place!

Heather Marshall (11)
Kingston Primary School, Benfleet

The War

I was told it was the last war,
There would not be another.
Until the phone call came,
it said, 'It's started up again.'
All the noise of screaming when
the bombs come falling down.
I thought it would be nice,
some peace in the world,
where buildings stay standing
and we could all stay alive,
But it never happened,
Yes is never happened.

Shaun Gayford (10)
Kingston Primary School, Benfleet

Be Thankful Lucky People

We are all guilty and you know it,
So you should admit it,
Think of other people,
Beside yourself,
And get on with life,
You need to learn the rules,
Aim high and be courageous in what you do,
Never waste your food, it's a week's worth of shopping,
Think of the poor in other places with no food.
So you should be thankful!

We are luckier than most people, so do things for others,
They could starve to death,
Think of this we are overloaded on the food we eat,
Every day we eat too much but other places they have nothing,
Remember to give and share all the time,
The poor have nothing to eat,
So be a thankful person,
Probably at this moment they are despondent,
Compare us to them,
Be grateful!

We have loads to eat,
But they only have crumbs,
Warm beds to lie in,
They have to lie on an ice-cold pavement,
The food they have is not a lot,
So the food we have is loads,
Think of how rich we are on our food,
Raindrops of tears lay in their eyes of hunger in the air,
Look at what we have.
Give some to the poor!

So why don't we think,
Before we shop,
Think before you buy things.
Let's pray and hope God gets the message we send to him for help!

Shannon Burton (10)
Kingston Primary School, Benfleet

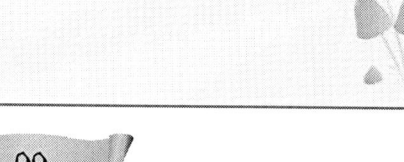

Harvest Poem

Leaves of yellow, orange and green.
One by one as leaves flutter in the breeze.
Harvest time is a time of thanks.
In consideration of our food bank.
Think of those who have less.
Harvest time of love God bless.

Benjamin Rackley (10)
Kingston Primary School, Benfleet

Message Of The Woods

Beautiful trees blowing in the wind,
Fresh air that we breathe.
How can they obliterate this?
It makes me so despondent.

Arched trees over my head
And leaves on the ground.
How dare they,
How can they?

I've been optimistic for my woods to stay.
However I may be beaten.
They put me through mental anguish,
What side shall I be on?

There's nothing hideous here.
However those imbeciles go through with the mistake.
How dare they,
How dare they?

Joel Wright (11)
Kingston Primary School, Benfleet

The Unexpected War

I am not quite sure why I am so sad,
this fault makes me so mad

Perhaps I didn't see this war coming so fast,
I hope it will soon be in the past.

I used to be in the army when I was younger,
but now I am a fish monger.

I got a phone call from the army and it said,
that my muscular younger cousin was dead!

I was really crying,
then after I kept on sighing.

That's what I was told
That's what I was told.

Sam Phillips (10)
Kingston Primary School, Benfleet

My Daddy

I was told Daddy had to leave to go to war
I never wanted him to go
But he kissed me on the forehead
It was time for him to go

He's up fighting day and night
I look for him in the morning
In war it must be a fright
I love him too much for him to die

One morning he walked in strong and tall
And what a lovely day it was
And what a lovely day it was.

Abigail Bush (10)
Kingston Primary School, Benfleet

Untitled

Why do we have banks of food and others have so little?
Why so we take our food for granted when others starve to death?
Why can't life be more fair and even?
Why don't we appreciate what we have?

A bunch of harvest whys, it's always been the same,
We must remember to give thanks
And share and never ever waste.

Sean Roe (10)
Kingston Primary School, Benfleet

Don't Bomb My House

Don't bomb my house,
The house is my home,
The cluttered room is my home,
The grandfather clock, the old chest of drawers
That my nan gave me the year before.
You ruined my sight the sight of my home,
How could you do that
I want you to go . . .
If you bomb my house, you bomb me too,
I'm not leaving, I'm not leaving
You will have to take me too.

Sally Logan (10)
Kingston Primary School, Benfleet

A Barracuda

Small and scaly
Caught daily.
River lovers
There it smothers.

Quick and speedy
Sharp teeth needy.
Wide or narrow
It'll eat a sparrow.

Piranha brothers
Lucky four-leaf clover.
Swarming round Dover
A barracuda.

Christian Lister (10)
Kingston Primary School, Benfleet

My Dad Set The Kitchen On Fire

My dad set the kitchen on fire,
He broke the tumble dryer!
When I tried to look,
He pretended to cook,
I wonder how much it will cost?

An hour later my mummy came home,
I want to know how she reacts,
Maybe she will cry,
She won't want to sign those contracts!

Daddy said it's not a problem,
Apart from the pans because he dropped them!

Jessica Mendies (10)
Kingston Primary School, Benfleet

The Zoo

One day when I went to the zoo,
I walked in and it smelled like animal poo.
I gagged and covered my nose in disgust,
It was a smell so bad it smelled like rust.
So I turned and walked up to a park ranger,
And I asked him although he was a stranger.
'Excuse me Sir, can you smell that smell?
It's really strange and it makes my nose ring like a bell!'

He said, 'Well actually yes I can,
It smells like what I'd cook after frying it in a pan.'
So he walked into the monkey enclosure.
I mean to walk in there is a deadly exposure.
So he looked round once, and he looked round twice,
Until he said . . . 'This doesn't smell very nice!'

Which was followed by, 'There's nothing over here . . .
Except the monkey's diarrhoea!'
He scooped it up with his trusty shovel,
By the looks of it, that monkey was in trouble.
And the smell hit me just once more,
But so much that I fell on the floor.

I don't go to that zoo anymore.

Joseph Greenwood (10)
Kingston Primary School, Benfleet

Maddie's Workshop

Featured Author:

Maddie Stewart

Maddie is a children's writer, poet and author who currently lives in Coney Island, Northern Ireland.

Maddie has 5 published children's books, 'Cinders', 'Hal's Sleepover', 'Bertie Rooster', 'Peg' and 'Clever Daddy'. Maddie uses her own unpublished work to provide entertaining, interactive poems and rhyming stories for use in her workshops with children when she visits schools, libraries, arts centres and book festivals. Favourites are 'Silly Billy, Auntie Millie' and 'I'm a Cool, Cool Kid'. Maddie works throughout Ireland from her home in County Down. She is also happy to work from a variety of bases in England. She has friends and family, with whom she regularly stays, in Leicester, Bedford, London and Ashford (Kent). Maddie's workshops are aimed at 5-11-year-olds. Check out Maddie's website for all her latest news and free poetry resources **www.maddiestewart.com**.

Read on to pick up some fab writing tips!

Nonsense Workshop

**If you find silliness fun,
you will love nonsense poems.
Nonsense poems might describe silly things,
or people, or situations,
or, any combination of the three.**

For example:

When I got out of bed today,
both my arms had run away.
I sent my feet to fetch them back.
When they came back, toe in hand
I realised what they had planned.
They'd made the breakfast I love most,
buttered spider's eggs on toast.

**One way to find out if you enjoy nonsense poems
is to start with familiar nursery rhymes.
Ask your teacher to read them out,
putting in the names of some children in your class.**

Like this: Troy and Jill went up the hill
to fetch a pail of water.
Troy fell down
and broke his crown
and Jill came tumbling after.

If anyone is upset at the idea of using their name, then don't use it.

Did you find this fun?

Maddie's Workshop

**Now try changing a nursery rhyme.
Keep the rhythm and the rhyme style, but invent a silly situation.**

Like this: Hickory Dickory Dare
a pig flew up in the air.
The clouds above
gave him a shove
Hickory Dickory Dare.

Or this: Little Miss Mabel
sat at her table
eating a strawberry pie
but a big, hairy beast
stole her strawberry feast
and made poor little Mabel cry.

How does your rhyme sound if you put your own name in it?

Another idea for nonsense poems is to pretend letters are people and have them do silly things.

For example:
| Mrs A | Mrs B | Mrs C |
| Lost her way | Dropped a pea | Ate a tree |

**To make your own 'Silly People Poem', think of a word to use.
To show you an example, I will choose the word 'silly'.
Write your word vertically down the left hand side of your page.
Then write down some words which rhyme
with the sound of each letter.**

S mess, dress, Bess, chess, cress
I eye, bye, sky, guy, pie, sky
L sell, bell, shell, tell, swell, well
L " " " " " " (" means the same as written above)
Y (the same words as those rhyming with I)

Use your rhyming word lists to help you make up your poem.

Mrs S made a mess
Mrs I ate a pie
Mrs L rang a bell
Mrs L broke a shell
Mrs Y said 'Bye-bye.'

**You might even make a 'Silly Alphabet' by using
all the letters of the alphabet.**

**It is hard to find rhyming words for all the letters.
H, X and W are letters which are hard to match with rhyming words.
I'll give you some I've thought of:**

> **H -** cage, stage, wage (close but not perfect)
> **X -** flex, specs, complex, Middlesex
> **W -** trouble you, chicken coop, bubble zoo

**However, with nonsense poems, you can use nonsense words.
You can make up your own words.**

**To start making up nonsense words you could
try mixing dictionary words together.
Let's make up some nonsense animals.**

Make two lists of animals. (You can include birds and fish as well.)

Your lists can be as long as you like. These are lists I made:

elephant	kangaroo
tiger	penguin
lizard	octopus
monkey	chicken

**Now use the start of an animal on one list and substitute
it for the start of an animal from your other list.**

I might use the start of oct/opus ... oct and substitute it for the end of l/izard
to give me a new nonsense animal ... an octizard.
I might swap the start of monk/ey ... monk with the end of kang/aroo
To give me another new nonsense animal ... a monkaroo.

What might a monkaroo look like? What might it eat?

**You could try mixing some food words in the same way,
to make up nonsense foods.**

cabbage	potatoes
lettuce	parsley
bacon	crisps

**Cribbage, bacley, and lettatoes are some nonsense foods
made up from my lists.**

Let's see if I can make a nonsense poem about my monkaroo.

My monkaroo loves bacley.
He'll eat lettatoes too
But his favourite food is cribbage
Especially if it's blue.

Would you like to try and make up your own nonsense poem?

**Nonsense words don't have to be a combination of dictionary words.
They can be completely 'made up'.
You can use nonsense words to write nonsense sonnets,
or list poems or any type of poem you like.**

Here is a poem full of nonsense words:

I melly micked a turdle
and flecked a pendril's tum.
I plotineyed a shugat
and dracked a pipin's plum.

**Ask your teacher to read it putting in some children's names instead
of the first I, and he or she instead of the second I.**

Did that sound funny?

You might think that nonsense poems are just silly and not for the serious poet. However poets tend to love language. Making up your own words is a natural part of enjoying words and sounds and how they fit together. Many poets love the freedom nonsense poems give them. Lots and lots of very famous poets have written nonsense poems. I'll name some: **Edward Lear**, **Roger McGough**, **Lewis Carroll**, **Jack Prelutsky** and **Nick Toczek**. Can you or your teacher think of any more? For help with a class nonsense poem or to find more nonsense nursery rhymes look on my website, **www.maddiestewart.com**. Have fun! Maddie Stewart.

Poetry Techniques

Here is a selection of poetry techniques with examples

Metaphors & Similes

A *metaphor* is when you describe your subject *as* something else, for example:
'Winter is a cruel master leaving the servants in a bleak wilderness'
whereas a *simile* describes your subject *like* something else i.e.
'His blue eyes are like ice-cold puddles' or 'The flames flickered like eyelashes'.

Personification

This is to simply give a personality to something that is not human, for example 'Fear spreads her uneasiness around' or 'Summer casts down her warm sunrays'.

Imagery

To use words to create mental pictures of what you are trying to convey, your poem should awaken the senses and make the reader feel like they are in that poetic scene ...
'The sky was streaked with pink and red as shadows cast across the once-golden sand'.
'The sea gently lapped the shore as the palm trees rustled softly in the evening breeze'.

Assonance & Alliteration

Alliteration uses a repeated constant sound and this effect can be quite striking:
'Smash, slippery snake slithered sideways'.
Assonance repeats a significant vowel or vowel sound to create an impact:
'The pool looked cool'.

Repetition

By repeating a significant word the echo effect can be a very powerful way of enhancing an emotion or point your poem is putting across.
'The blows rained down, down,
Never ceasing,
Never caring
About the pain,
The pain'.

Onomatopoeia

This simply means you use words that sound like the noise you are describing, for example 'The rain *pattered* on the window' or 'The tin can *clattered* up the alley'.

Rhythm & Metre

The *rhythm* of a poem means 'the beat', the sense of movement you create. The placing of punctuation and the use of syllables affect the *rhythm* of the poem. If your intention is to have your poem read slowly, use double, triple or larger syllables and punctuate more often, where as if you want to have a fast-paced read use single syllables, less punctuation and shorter sentences.
If you have a regular rhythm throughout your poem this is known as *metre*.

Enjambment

This means you don't use punctuation at the end of your line, you simply let the line flow on to the next one. It is commonly used and is a good word to drop into your homework!

Tone & Lyric

The poet's intention is expressed through their *tone*. You may feel happiness, anger, confusion, loathing or admiration for your poetic subject. Are you criticising or praising? How you feel about your topic will affect your choice of words and therefore your *tone*. For example 'I *loved* her', 'I *cared* for her', 'I *liked* her'.
If you write the poem from a personal view or experience this is referred to as a *lyrical* poem. A good example of a lyrical poem is Seamus Heaney's 'Mid-term Break' or any sonnet!

All About Shakespeare

Try this fun quiz with your family, friends or even in class!

1. Where was Shakespeare born?

....

2. Mercutio is a character in which Shakepeare play?

....

3. Which monarch was said to be 'quite a fan' of his work?

....

4. How old was he when he married?

....

5. What is the name of the last and 'only original' play he wrote?

....

6. What are the names of King Lear's three daughters?

....

7. Who is Anne Hathaway?

....

All About Shakespeare

8. Which city is the play 'Othello' set in?

....

9. Can you name 2 of Shakespeare's 17 comedies?

....

10. 'This day is call'd the feast of Crispian: He that outlives this day, and comes safe home, Will stand a tip-toe when this day is nam'd, and rouse him at the name of Crispian' is a quote from which play?

....

11. Leonardo DiCaprio played Romeo in the modern day film version of Romeo and Juliet. Who played Juliet in the movie?

....

12. Three witches famously appear in which play?

....

13. Which famous Shakespearean character is Eric in the image to the left?

....

14. What was Shakespeare's favourite poetic form?

....

Answers are printed on the last page of the book, good luck!

If you would rather try the quiz online,
you can do so at www.youngwriters.co.uk.

Poetry Activity

Word Soup

To help you write a poem, or even a story, on any theme, you should create word soup!

If you have a theme or subject for your poem, base your word soup on it.
If not, don't worry, the word soup will help you find a theme.

To start your word soup you need ingredients:

- Nouns (names of people, places, objects, feelings, i.e. Mum, Paris, house, anger)
- Colours
- Verbs ('doing words', i.e. kicking, laughing, running, falling, smiling)
- Adjectives (words that describe nouns, i.e. tall, hairy, hollow, smelly, angelic)

We suggest at least 5 of each from the above list, this will make sure your word soup has plenty of choice. Now, if you have already been given a theme or title for your poem, base your ingredients on this. If you have no idea what to write about, write down whatever you like, or ask a teacher or family member to give you a theme to write about.

Poetry Activity

Making Word Soup

Next, you'll need a sheet of paper.
Cut it into at least 20 pieces. Make sure the pieces are big enough to write your ingredients on, one ingredient on each piece of paper.
Write your ingredients on the pieces of paper.
Shuffle the pieces of paper and put them all in a box or bowl
- something you can pick the paper out of without looking at the words.
Pick out 5 words to start and use them to write your poem!

Example:

Our theme is winter. Our ingredients are:
- Nouns: snowflake, Santa, hat, Christmas, snowman.
- Colours: blue, white, green, orange, red.
- Verbs: ice-skating, playing, laughing, smiling, wrapping.
- Adjectives: cold, tall, fast, crunchy, sparkly.

**Our word soup gave us these 5 words:
snowman, red, cold, hat, fast and our poem goes like this:**

It's a *cold* winter's day,
My nose and cheeks are *red*
As I'm outside, building my *snowman*,
I add a *hat* and a carrot nose to finish,
I hope he doesn't melt too *fast*!

**Tip: add more ingredients to your word soup
and see how many different poems you can write!**

**Tip: if you're finding it hard to write a poem with
the words you've picked, swap a word with another one!**

**Tip: try adding poem styles and techniques,
such as assonance or haiku to your soup for an added challenge!**

SCRIBBLER!

*If you enjoy creative writing then you'll love our magazine, Scribbler!, the fun and educational magazine for 7-11-year-olds that works alongside Key Stage 2 National Literacy Strategy Learning Objectives. For further information visit **www.youngwriters.co.uk**.*

Grammar Fun
Our resident dinosaur Bernard helps to improve writing skills from punctuation to spelling.

Nessie's Workshop
Each issue Nessie explains a style of writing and sets an exercise for you to do. Previous workshops include the limerick, haiku and shape poems.

Awesome Author
Read all about past and present authors. Previous Awesome Authors include Roald Dahl, William Shakespeare and Ricky Gervais!

Once Upon a Time ...
Lord Oscar starts a story ... it's your job to finish it. Our favourite wins a writing set.

Guest Author
A famous author drops by and answers some of our in-depth questions, while donating a great prize to give away. Recent authors include former Children's Laureate Michael Morpurgo, adventurer Bear Grylls and Nick Ward, author of the Charlie Small Journals.

Art Gallery
Send Bizzy your paintings and drawings and his favourite wins an art set including some fab Staedtler goodies.

Puzzle Time!
Could you find Eric? Unscramble Anna Gram's words? Tackle our hard puzzles? If so, winners receive fab prizes.

The Brainiacs
Scribbler!'s own gang of wiz kids are always on hand to help with spellings, alternative words and writing styles, they'll get you on the right track!

Prizes
Every issue we give away fantastic prizes. Recent prizes include Staedtler goodies, signed copies of Bear Grylls' books and posters, signed copies of Ricky Gervais' books, Charlie Small goodie bags, family tickets to The Eden Project, The Roald Dahl Museum & Story Centre and Alton Towers, a digital camera, books and writing sets galore and many other fab prizes!

... plus much more!
We keep you up to date with all the happenings in the world of literature, including blog updates from the Children's Laureate.

*If you are too old for Scribbler! magazine or have an older friend who enjoys creative writing, then check out Wordsmith. Wordsmith is for 11-18-year-olds and is jam-packed full of brilliant features, young writers' work, competitions and interviews too. For further information check out **www.youngwriters.co.uk** or ask an adult to call us on (01733) 890066.*

To get an adult to subscribe to either magazine for you, ask them to visit the website or give us a call.

Outside In The Garden

Winter's chill of frosted leaves,
It's cold, it is dark,
Shivers and shakes,
Dogs and ditches,
Leaves and trees,
This is the beauty we will leave.

Connor Wallington (10)
Kingston Primary School, Benfleet

Harvest Poem

Why do we have everything and they have nothing?

Why do they live on the street and we live in safe houses?

Why do we have lovely food and they
have absolutely disgusting food?

Why, why, why?

Reece McAnulty (10)
Kingston Primary School, Benfleet

Foxes

Foxes are quick
Foxes are slight, you can only see one
sometimes with the naked eye.

Be careful if you see one they might attack.
Sharp teeth, vicious claws,
no matter what if it pounces watch out
there's more about hiding,
waiting for the right moment to strike their foe.

You'll never hear from their victim ever again.

George Norris (10)
Kingston Primary School, Benfleet

Why?

Why would I?
Why would I not?
Why? Why? Why?
I don't know why.
Why would I?
Why do I?
Why do you?
Why do you lie?
Why would I?

Jasmine Carrier (9)
Magdalen Gates Primary School, Norwich

Cats

Flea on cat, cat on flea
Cats like you and kittens like me
Kittens like playing and cats like I
Sometimes have a twinkle in their eye
Kittens like chicken and cats like fish
And sometimes they have it with gravy, delish!
Cats have paws and kittens have claws
And usually they try to break the laws!
Cats and kittens love to sleep
And now it's time for them to count some sheep
My cat and kitten are fast asleep
Curling up together in a sweet little heap.

Niamh Canny (10)
Magdalen Gates Primary School, Norwich

Mischievous Cats

Cats are mischievous
They are crazy.
They like chasing chickens
That are lazy.
I like computer games.
All day up and down
I like playing in my tree house,
I could do it all day
Every day.

Ruben Price (9)
Magdalen Gates Primary School, Norwich

Nan's

At my nan's I feel so cosy
Her stew is tasty
Being in her arms is lovely
Seeing Tinker, the dog, makes me happy.

Home
Warm
Good food
Big garden
Comfortable.

Jordan Rhys Townsend (10)
Magdalen Gates Primary School, Norwich

Food

Spaghetti, spaghetti, as long as a snake
Pasta, pasta, as curly as a spring
Meatballs, meatballs, as round as a football
Mars bars, Mars bars, as creamy as a Galaxy
And I can't forget potatoes, I love them.

Devon Dray (10)
Magdalen Gates Primary School, Norwich

The Mad House

I smell the cooking that my mum does for me.
Our kitten goes mad as she climbs for my tea.
My hamster goes crazy as she climbs to the bars
And my fish are relaxed and calm.
I waved out the window to my friends outside.
I went to bed and rested my head.
In the morning clothes were laid for me.
It was a rosy red dress.
I played in my room until ten.
I went into the kitchen and my mum was in bed.
I went outside and our house was red!

Hannah Cooper (9)
Magdalen Gates Primary School, Norwich

Music

I love to spin my wheels on the record player
In my awesome house I love to crash those symbols
In my drumming room I crash and smash those drums
And when the day is done I climb up on my bed
And I slide down my slide
And climb up on top and slowly doze off.

Joe Kirman (9)
Magdalen Gates Primary School, Norwich

In The Different Rooms

In the kitchen I get told
'Stop throwing jelly at the telly'
'Ketchup on your cornflakes, that's disgusting'
'Food in your shoes, stop being silly'
'Don't throw noodles on the poodles'
'Do the washing up'
'Do not break that cup'
'Ludo brought in earthworms again go clear it up'
In the living room I get told
'Hoover the dust, it gives your dad a cold'
I turn on the telly for a quick relax
And my fat cat Ludo joins me
I smell the smell of cooking spaghetti
I go into the kitchen for my tea
Then it's off to bed where my head hits the pillow
And my room fills with zzzzzzzzzz.

Mina Mitchell-Hardy (9)
Magdalen Gates Primary School, Norwich

Scott The Mad Dog

When I step out of the train I hear the familiar bark,
The bark of Scott, the mad dog, wanting to go to the park.
We have got a long drive back to my grandma's house
and when we get there I'm greeted by a pounce,
From Scott the very mad dog.
I expect we will go on a long walk and my mum and grandma
will just talk, talk and talk
Scott, the mad dog, barking all the time.

Maia Kemp-Welch (10)
Magdalen Gates Primary School, Norwich

Recycle

R euse things that you don't need.
E ven adults can use the car less.
C an you have your own bags rather than shops bags?
Y ou can save the world too!
C areful you don't put things in the bin that can be recycled.
L et's stop polluting the Earth, so we can save it.
E ven though we're children we can help recycle.

Michael Norton (10)
Newlands Primary School, Ramsgate

Doing Our Bit To Help The Planet

Doing our bit to help the planet,
Recycling an old tin can,
Come on we all live in Thanet,
The next step is to fill a van.

Whether it's big, small
Or tiny enough to fit in a box,
Your contribution will make a change after all,
It could even save a fox.

Please respect our world,
You can only do your best,
Please help our world,
And think about the rest!

Summer Gadd (10)
Newlands Primary School, Ramsgate

Recycling

R escue the world and stop pollution
E co warriors save the word
C hange the way you treat the planet
Y ou won't want the world to end
C hange the way you pollute
L eave animals to do their thing
E co warriors stop people polluting.

Charlotte Shorter Coombes (10)
Newlands Primary School, Ramsgate

Fire, Water And Wind

Fire's a powerful thing, so is water and wind,
They can do anything they want,
Controlled by God and the heavens,
Power ruling Earth and the people today and right now.
Fire burning woods and forests destroying habitats and life,
Water waves crashing on the sand making great big sand dunes,
Wind blowing from side to side making tornados and hurricanes.

Oliver Annis (10)
Newlands Primary School, Ramsgate

I Will Put Into The Box
(Inspired by 'Magic Box' by Kit Wright)

I will put into the box . . .
a scaly fish swimming a long river,
I will put into the box . . .
a furry fox walking down town
I will put into the box . . .
a genie so shiny that you need sunglasses on!

Jack Taylor (10)
Newlands Primary School, Ramsgate

My Box
(Inspired by 'Magic Box' by Kit Wright)

I would put into my box . . .
a magical world where people fly and are cheerful!

I would put into my box . . .
a mystical corner full of trees and strange creatures
that lurk in and out and amongst.

I would have in my box . . .
all the things that make my day
like the golden sun
and having a great time with my friends.

Cameron Sanham (11)
Newlands Primary School, Ramsgate

This Little Globe

This little globe is my only home,
My only chance to get things right,
But luckily, if we treat it well,
It won't die overnight.

Olivia Martin (10)
Newlands Primary School, Ramsgate

Magic Box
(Inspired by 'Magic Box' by Kit Wright)

I will put in my box . . .
snowflakes that fall to the cold, frozen floor
and sparkles, that light up the sky, like a painting.

I will put in my box . . .
a picture of people dancing in the moonlight
and videos of a baby for the first time.

I will put in my box . . .
a picture of the sun setting on a beautiful day
and stars twinkling like diamonds in the sky.

Katie McCullough (10)
Newlands Primary School, Ramsgate

The Magic Box
(Inspired by 'Magic Box' by Kit Wright)

I will put in my box . . .
Marvellous money and magical mates
Shimmery sunshine, blasting boats
Enormous elephant, tiny tigers
Gambling games, glittering gold
Shooting stars and spaceships spinning
Snoring and sleeping sausages
The green grass and hairy horses.

James Bennett (10)
Newlands Primary School, Ramsgate

Football

'F oul,' said the player on the floor
'O ff side,' shouted the player running
'O uch,' shouted the player kicked in the leg
T ackle him before he scores
B oom, what a goal to draw
A s he scores he falls over
'L inesman . . . it was offside,' shouted the player
L ook it is a skilful goal . . . the winner.

Marcus Baldwin (10)
Newlands Primary School, Ramsgate

The Magic Box
(Based on 'Magic Box' by Kit Wright)

I will put in my box . . .
An owl's voice echoing down the dark, gloomy wood
A small new baby's first ever tiny squeaky laugh
The vicious fast wind zooming past my shoulder

I will put in my box . . .
The vision of a pale white horse galloping on a cold winter's day
The breath that lies deep within my soul.

Cerys Haine (10)
Newlands Primary School, Ramsgate

Recycle

R euse our baskets,
E co-warrior saves the planet,
C ans can be recycled,
Y ell to the world, 'Recycle our plastic bags,'
C leaners are sorting out bottles to put in the bottle bank,
L et the world recycle, reuse and reduce,
E nergy can be saved!

Georgia Dooney (10)
Newlands Primary School, Ramsgate

Recycle

R ummaging through my cousin's drawers to bring old clothes alive.
E mptying plastic bottles into the green bin to survive
C arrying on the people are, we will not last
Y es to the people, care and share,
   the environment that we live in.
C an you stop pollution around and can you recycle each day?
L et us think of the damage we have caused
E ventually we will all say . . .
   Hip hip hooray!

Chelsea Usher (10)
Newlands Primary School, Ramsgate

The Robin In The Tree

Once I saw a robin perched in a tree.
It looked as if it was smiling at me.
I saw in his nest a shiny bright key.
It sat in the tree and watched me.
There jumped Ginger the fat cat.
He was so funny you could use him as a hat.
He jumped up at Robin, hoping to have him for his tea.
But accidently missed and fell out the tree.

Cassandra Thatcher (9)
Pickhurst Junior School, West Wickham

Roller Coaster

On the roller coaster as we get in,
All of a sudden we started to spin,
Up, down, round and round,
I could feel my heart start to pound.
As we went up slowly, slowly,
My tummy did a roly-poly,
Then it happened, out of the blue,
All of a sudden we were going down, 'Woohoo!'
Faster, faster, we couldn't stop,
Then my tummy did a funny flop,
I couldn't stop myself but scream,
My smile was not happy, not even a beam.
When it was over I could barely talk,
I was relieved I could even walk,
I had had enough for one day,
We could finally go home, hip hip hooray.

Isabelle Secord (9)
Pickhurst Junior School, West Wickham

Red

Red is bright
Red is mercy
Red can be death
Red is joy
Red is always.

Henry Allen (10)
Pickhurst Junior School, West Wickham

Lost In Space

Once I went into space
I forgot to tie my lace
So I tripped over into space,
I was lost in planet Tros.
I did not know where I was
Because I was lost in Tros.
But then I saw Earth with a purse.
How strange was that?
But then I saw a bat that was that,
So I went back on Earth
And everyone had a purse.

Stanley Mattless (9)
Pickhurst Junior School, West Wickham

Untitled

Red flower called rose and it smells like strawberry
Feel great to touch, like melting ice cream.
Orangey carrots like my cat's fur.
Cabbages like sparkly green grass
Cabbages crunch, soft layers of pizza.
Chips, the gorgeous, spicy, crispy chip.
Fish the undersea creature, crunchy batter, yummy fish.
Sweetcorn that some people like but some hate.
All of this food is good for you.

Jacob Taylor-Green (10)
Queen's Hill Primary School, Norwich

How I Love Tennis

Oh tennis, tennis, tennis.
I just love it,
I hit and whack the ball
Not forgetting I'm the best of all.
My mum and dad call me bad and say,
'Be careful with that ball!'

Ola Krukowka
Queen's Hill Primary School, Norwich

Animals

A nimals can be cute and fluffy
N ot all animals can be pets
I know somebody who had a pet lion
M any people think he is dead
A lthough he is as lively as always
L iving the high life
S ame as always.

Isobel Wilkinson
Queen's Hill Primary School, Norwich

My Family

My mum and dad are not so bad
They have six children
They must be mad

My older brother is 12 years old
He's always on his DS
Playing on Pokémon Gold

Then there's my sister
She's younger than me
Always singing and dancing
A Hannah Montana wannabe

Next are my 2 brothers
Their hair is bright ginger
They play on the trampoline
Pretending to be a ninja

Last but not least
Comes Baby Samuel
He's my favourite
Out of them all.

Megan White
Queen's Hill Primary School, Norwich

Gymnastics Poem

I love gymnastics it's so cool
Can't wait to go there after school

My mummy calls me Bendy Wendy
And my kit is super trendy

I've been going since I was four
I just can't wait to get through that door

I have a mate
That also thinks it's really great
I have another mate
That started when she was eight
How great

We're the best
And together we can beat the rest
We're obsessed to take on the rest

I have got a bronze
I have got a gold
But all I want is a trophy that is bold.

Ebonhi Andrews (10)
Queen's Hill Primary School, Norwich

Zorro

Z ooming through the land on his trusty horse Toronado
O n missions he's a hero but if he doesn't have his mask he's just like you and me.
R ound and
R ound he goes looking for adventure.
O ver the hills he rides on his shimmering black horse.

Abi Lloyd (10)
Queen's Hill Primary School, Norwich

Popcorn

P opcorn, popcorn
O ozing with toffee
P opping popcorn popping in a pan
C orn goes pop with a very loud bang
O rbiting around, around in the pan
R ound and bobbly
N ice and nobbly, popcorn is the best!

Georgia Coulthard & Alyssa Newton
Queen's Hill Primary School, Norwich

Gills
(Inspired by 'If I Had Wings' by Pie Corbett)

If I had gills
I would explore the ocean
And swim with glittering turtles with shining shells.

If I had gills
I would walk on water
And catch some fish.

If I had gills
I would touch the dolphin's grey, smooth skin
And a starfish on its back.

If I had gills
I would taste some fish
And feel a clownfish.

If I had gills
I would dream of not having gills
And I would dream of tasting the fresh air.

Addison Malkinson (9)
Redcastle Furze Primary School, Thetford

Gills
(Inspired by 'If I Had Wings' by Pie Corbett)

If I had gills
I would touch the fluff of the surf.

If I had gills
I would taste a massive bite of the coral.

If I had gills
I would gaze at the fish
Yellow as the sun.

Byron Brown (9)
Redcastle Furze Primary School, Thetford

Gills
(Inspired by 'If I Had Wings' by Pie Corbett)

If I had gills
I would taste a chunk of coral
from the deep blue sea.

If I had gills
I would like the sea breeze
cooling me.

If I had gills
I would look at the stars all night long.

If I had gills
I would touch the ocean
spitting out foam.

Max Dimon (9)
Redcastle Furze Primary School, Thetford

Tail
(Inspired by 'If I Had Wings' by Pie Corbett)

If I had a tail
I would balance on trees like monkeys
and break the world record for the highest tree climb.

If I had a tail
I would bounce up and down on it,
and curl it up and use it as a pillow.

If I had a tail,
I would touch the fingertips of the trees
and I would see the world from the top of the jungle.

Joao Lampreia (9)
Redcastle Furze Primary School, Thetford

Gills
(Inspired by 'If I Had Wings' by Pie Corbett)

If I had gills
I would touch the pointed coral leaves.

If I had gills
I would taste a piece of the food
People throw in the sea.

If I had gills
I would listen to the dolphins sing
Like never before.

If I had gills
I would smell the salty water.

Ruby Dean (10)
Redcastle Furze Primary School, Thetford

Gills
(Inspired by 'If I Had Wings' by Pie Corbett)

If I had gills
I would touch the fingertips of the coral reef.

If I had gills
I would taste the leftovers of the people on the beach.

If I had gills
I would smell the smooth crunchy seaweed.

If I had gills
I would smell the fresh air in the deep blue sea.

If I had gills
I would hear the squeaky dolphins talk to each other.

Jordan Hampton (9)
Redcastle Furze Primary School, Thetford

My Trip To Africa
(Inspired by 'Refuelling' by Valerie Bloom)

My call is back to Africa,
Where my childhood was placed.

I find my passport
Jump on the shiny, loud plane
Wondering what smells and sounds I will discover.

Finally I reach my destination,
Eventually making it on an enormous red bus
Glowing like the sun setting.

Hopping nervously off the bus
Flabbergasted by the vast country
I could feel the hot air shooting at me.
Now I was back in my childhood.

Abby Fendley (9)
Redcastle Furze Primary School, Thetford

What I Would Do If I Had Four Legs, Wings And Gills
(Inspired by 'If I Had Wings' by Pie Corbett)

If I had four legs
I would run all day.
If I had four legs
I would run to Australia for the winter.
If I had four legs
I would run to the shops and back
In a second.

But if I had wings
I would see all the little people.
If I had wings
I would sleep on the clouds.
If I had wings
I would glide through the sky.
If I had wings
I would be as delicate as a ballerina.

But if I had gills
I would shake hands with an octopus.
If I had gills
I would prance around all day.
If I had gills
I would race a dolphin and still win.
If I had gills
I would gaze at the dark blue sky.

And that's what I would do
If I had four legs, wings and gills.

Levi Strutton (10)
Redcastle Furze Primary School, Thetford

Fins
(Inspired by 'If I Had Wings' by Pie Corbett)

If I had fins
I would taste salty water
And swim like a shark

If I had fins
I would touch a dolphin
Swimming past.

If I had fins
I would swim with turtles like small, glittering rocks
And feel some sandy rocks.

If I had fins
I would explore the ocean
And swim with lots of mermaids, sharks and blue whales.

If I had fins
I would collect some pebbles and starfish
For my collection.

If I had fins
I would live in the ocean
In the clear blue sea
And feel the breeze on me.

Thomas Hazelden (9)
Redcastle Furze Primary School, Thetford

Gills
(Inspired by 'If I Had Wings' by Pie Corbett)

If I had gills
I would touch
The rough coral reef.

If I had gills
I would swim to the bottom of the ocean
Like a shark trying to catch its prey.

If I had gills
I would swim to the lost city of Atlantis
To see spectacular, beautiful goldfish.

If I had gills
I would launch myself to the whales
To brush their jerking, gleaming grey skin.

If I had gills
I would swish through the ocean
Hearing the saltwater catch my hair.

If I had gills
I would twist and twirl
All around the world
Like a diver in a show.

Krystina Davis (9)
Redcastle Furze Primary School, Thetford

In The Year 2008
(Inspired by 'Refuelling' by Valerie Bloom)

I can hear a voice telling me
That I'm going on holiday,
But I wasn't sure who it was
Or what it was telling me.

The voice swirled around me,
And suddenly I was in the sky
Glimpsing Lego cities through the glass rectangle
As we speed through the cotton-wool clouds.

Eventually the plane landed.
My excitement grew
Surrounded by busy people.
Luggage collected and off we went.

Finally I reached my destination.
I could smell cut grass
I could see gorgeous roses
Growing out of the ground.
I could taste the adventures
About to begin.

Jazmine Louise Riley (9)
Redcastle Furze Primary School, Thetford

The Rusty Switch

I'm a switch, a rusty switch,
I'm alone.
I'm sad.
I'm alive.
No one ever sees me.
No one ever uses me
I stand against the wall, waiting for someone to
Touch me.
Hold me.
Use me.
I'm the switch, the rusty switch.
One day it happened.
My heart raced.
Someone touched me.
Held me.
Used me.
I screamed, I laughed, I smiled.
I'm the switch, the happy switch.
I get used and I'm funny.
I'm not alone.
I'm not sad
But I'm alive.

Lauren Bibby (10)
Roach Vale Primary School, Colchester

The Rolling Waves

The rolling waves in the gusty wind.
The rolling waves pouncing through the darkness,
At the heart of the waves slicing through the rocks.
The jagged waves lapping across the cliffs.
Jagged waves crashing into the old jagged cliff
Crashing into the ocean.
The children getting flown by kites
And the sandcastles that children built.

Luke Heffron (10)
Roach Vale Primary School, Colchester

The Blue Ocean

The ocean is a terrifying tiger,
It drags in its prey with its sharp, pointy, white teeth.
It pulls in stones with its claws all day until it's dark.
When it's dark it just rolls on the beach as it sleeps.
The waves fall calm until morning.
When it wakes up the waves crash, the tiger has lots of secrets
that have not been touched.
The tiger sees more and more people every day as they
lay on the soft sand.
The tiger just stares at them all day long until they go.
The stones that the tiger pulls in with its claws just shatter
until there is nothing left.

Elise Jones (10)
Roach Vale Primary School, Colchester

The Hidden Tiger

The rogue waves pounced,
Clashing its jaws on the rugged cliffs,
Foaming blood soared into the distance.
He lunged forward to unexpecting prey,
Its tail lashed out, playing with his miniscule toys.
His tongue lolled in the hot, sandy days,
Happily waving at passing fish,
Strolling magnificently through the open world,
Resting in the cooling breeze.
Filling my momentous blue coat.

Tommy McWhirter (10)
Roach Vale Primary School, Colchester

The Fierce Sea

The mighty lion prowls the shore.
He pounced onto the rocks.
As he stretches, full of rage as he tumbles down heavily,
He moves slowly to the cliffs but before he does
He finds prey and attacks it
He is a spitfire,
Killer
And a destroyer
But as morning awakes he goes out.

Harrison Goulding (10)
Roach Vale Primary School, Colchester

The Mighty Sea

The mighty leopard prowls the shores,
He cruises everything in his path.
In the night he wrecks and he roars,
As he moves up the shores.
He crashes and thrashes against the colossal cliffs,
Forcing them to shatter.
He preys on the storm,
Using it to make him stronger,
Rougher,
Tougher.
He cracks and whacks the pointy rocks.
In the day he acts all calm and careless,
But secretly,
He's the deadly predator,
The sea,
The mighty sea.

Charlie Robinson (10)
Roach Vale Primary School, Colchester

Lucy Dog

Glossy jet-black fur,
Do not stir because
She will pounce,
Without doubt
Please do not shout
Get off her bed
Or she will stay
Until you pay.
Every day
When she does walk
Bark, bark, bark
She likes to talk
With a snuffle and a snort
She combs the trees
Chasing
Sheep, sticks and bumblebees.

Dylan Abraham (10)
Roach Vale Primary School, Colchester

The Waves

I am the screaming waves
The wild blue
The diving sea
I am the stormy ocean
The crashing deep
The monstrous menace
I am the powerful ocean
The plummeting dolphin
The motionless monster
I am
The
Wonderful.

Kieran Phillips (10)
Roach Vale Primary School, Colchester

Halloween Night

It's Halloween night
as I sit by my door
and wait for the frights
that the kids have in store

First a small ghost
who shivers and shakes
they rattle their chains
and demand sweets and cakes

Next is a goblin
small and green
I hold back my laugh
but give out a scream

Last is a witch
the best of them all
she's off to a party
a great Halloween ball.

Abigail Sample (7)
Rushmere Hall Primary School, Ipswich

Blue

Blue is the colour of the bright sky
Blue is the colour of our school uniform
Blue is the colour of Aidan's old trainers
Blue is the colour of the stripes on the tea towel
Blue is the colour of the trampoline
Blue is the colour of our school book bags
Blue is the colour of Mummy's folder
Blue is the colour of my fish bowl
Blue is the colour of a bright pen
Blue is the colour of an outside bin
Blue is Aidan's favourite colour.

Melissa Neale (7)
Rushmere Hall Primary School, Ipswich

Yellow

Yellow is the colour of the bright sun
Yellow is the colour of a delicate fairy's wings
Yellow is the colour of smooth hair
Yellow is the colour of an elegant dress
Yellow is the colour of messy paint
Yellow is the colour of a star shining bright
Yellow is the colour of a Labrador
Yellow is the colour of a light from up high
Yellow is the colour of a squishy banana.

Chloe Louise Last (7)
Rushmere Hall Primary School, Ipswich

Patrick

Patrick is my teddy bear
the best forever and ever

His head is very floppy
and it makes him very cuddly

Patrick's very hairy
but he isn't very scary

His fur is a creamy colour
and it's fluffy and nice

When he is smelly
he gets put in the washing machine
and then he hangs by his ears
on the washing line.

When I cuddle Patrick
I feel happy.

Jordan Campbell (7)
Rushmere Hall Primary School, Ipswich

Green

Green is the colour of crunchy green leaves.
Green is the colour of fresh, wet, smooth grass.
Green is the colour of plants.
Green is the colour of a car.
Green is the colour of a painting.
Green is the colour of Dad's wheelbarrow.
Green is the colour of a shiny wet bush.

Mia Blackman (7)
Rushmere Hall Primary School, Ipswich

Stars In The Sky

There are lots of stars in the sky.
There is a golden star,
A silver star and even a sparkling star.
I have never seen this many stars in the sky.
There is even a shining star
There are too many stars in the sky.
I have seen a shining, sparkling, golden, silver star
And there are so, so many stars
And there are more that I can spot.

Francesca Roberts (7)
Rushmere Hall Primary School, Ipswich

Rainbow

I see, I see a rainbow up in the air
Orange, purple, pink, green, black, yellow and blue
They are all nice colours
Can you guess how the sky makes a rainbow?
Rain and sun, that's why it's called a rainbow
Would you reach a rainbow in the sky?
The answer would be no.

Deimante Miceviciute (7)
Rushmere Hall Primary School, Ipswich

Space And Mars

Rockets flying, space carts racing,
The moon is disappearing.
Aliens playing, hovercraft floating,
Mars is breathing.
Satellites' signals spinning,
Martians walking
And I am drawing,
Neil Armstrong space walking,
Edwin Aldrin scanning Mars is boring,
But everyone is sporting.
But I know space is the best place for me.

Shalom Shibi (8)
Rushmere Hall Primary School, Ipswich

Blue

Blue is the sea in hot, hot Spain.
Blue is the colour of the falling rain.
Blue is as cold as ice.
Do you like blue? Yes it's nice.
Blue is in the rainbow in the sky above me way up high.
Blue is my school uniform I wear every day.
Bluebells are blue which you see in May.
I love the colour blue, do you?

Harriet Rush (8)
Rushmere Hall Primary School, Ipswich

School Of Colour

Rushmere Hall is the best school.
I like it because it's cool!
It's full of colour.
It's full of fun
And I can't wait till the half-term

I'll go swimming and I'll keep winning
And I'll keep singing.
The birds are tweeting in my ear,
That means they're having fun up there!

Emily Gallant (8)
Rushmere Hall Primary School, Ipswich

Animals

Horses clop
Rabbits hop

Kittens pounce
Puppies bounce

Worms wriggle
Monkeys giggle

Mice creep
Lions leap

Leopards stalk
But -
I walk.

Phoebe Dodd (8)
Rushmere Hall Primary School, Ipswich

My Cat

My cat is black
my cat is white
my cat loves fish
my cat is furry
my cat loves chicken
my cat is black
my cat is white
my cat loves me
my cat is a girl
my cat has had kittens
that were black and white
just like my cat!

Eden Upson (8)
Rushmere Hall Primary School, Ipswich

Summertime

The sun shines yellow
The skies are blue
Clouds are white and fluffy too
Birds sing sweetly
Bees buzz about
Butterflies flap about
In different colours, shapes and sizes
They never fail to surprise us.

Kaylee Meekings (8)
Rushmere Hall Primary School, Ipswich

My Family

A mum is cuddly
A mum is kind
A mum is happy
A mum is always cheerful

A dad is busy
A dad is kind
A dad is jolly
I'm so glad he's mine

A sister is annoying
A sister is a pleasure
A sister is thoughtful
A sister is a friend forever.

Bobby Crowhurst (8)
Rushmere Hall Primary School, Ipswich

Blue

Blue is the colour of my school jumper
Blue is the colour of this pen
Blue is the colour of a book bag
Blue is the colour of the sea
Blue is the colour of the sky when it's sunny
Blue can be made into different colours
Blue is the colour of my pyjamas
Blue is also my favourite colour.

Cameron Cornthwaite (8)
Rushmere Hall Primary School, Ipswich

Once Upon A Crazy Rhyme

Though you've heard once upon a time
This is something of a different rhyme
There lays Sleeping Beauty having a nap,
When over flies Captain Smarty Pants
Who gives her a zap!

Up she shoots like a rocket in the sky
But turns blue and green with big stripy eyes!
'Woah!' cries Captain, 'what shall I do?'
So he zapped her back to sleep and off he flew!

Jayden Novak (8)
Rushmere Hall Primary School, Ipswich

Ocean

The ocean is calm
The ocean is wild
Glistening fish swim through the coral reef
Up, down, turning and whirling through the ocean.
Hiding from the shark with its sharp, shining teeth ruling the ocean.
That is how the ocean is calm and wild!

Laura Towler (8)
Rushmere Hall Primary School, Ipswich

A Peacock's Tail

I saw a peacock with a tail
As red as hot lava
As green as an iguana
As blue as clear sparkling water

Like a crunchy apple
Like a pile of fresh green grass
Like a person's eyes looking at you

Look at the peacock's tail
What do you see?
I see a bright sparkly rainbow looking at me.

Paige James (9)
Rushmere Hall Primary School, Ipswich

A Halloween Night

Witches, wizards, ghosts and ghouls
Banging on your door,
Shouting trick or treat at you
We want more.

Witches, wizards, ghosts and ghouls,
Walking around with stuffed bags,
Full of chocolate, lollies and sweets
And all kinds of treats.

Witches, wizards, ghosts and ghouls,
Even zombies, pumpkins, spiders, skeletons and vampires!
Wandering around, knocking doors, ringing bells
Waiting for treats, we want more, we want more
We want more!

Esha Khan (9)
Rushmere Hall Primary School, Ipswich

A Peacock's Tail

In a peacock's tail I can see . . .
Red as a tomato
Green as a cucumber
Blue as the sky

Like a strawberry
Like a patch of grass
Like the sea

I see a cloud
I see a banana
I see a rubber
I see a sport
I see a letter
I see a scratch
I see a number
I see a bulb
I see a paper
I see a shoe
I see a TV
I see a book.

Mashiat Anwar (9)
Rushmere Hall Primary School, Ipswich

A Peacock's Tail

In a peacock's tail I can see . . .

Red, as red as a rose
Blue, as blue as our school uniform
Green, as green as a football pitch

Like a fire engine
Like the sea
Like a hedge

Look at the peacock's tail, what do you see?

I see a rainbow of eyes
I see a mouth, swallowing me up.

Manraj Digpal (9)
Rushmere Hall Primary School, Ipswich

A Peacock's Tail

In a peacock's tail I can see . . .
Grey, as grey as a rock,
Red, as red as lava,
Purple, as purple as damson jam,
Green, as green as ivy

Like a rose
Like a violet
Like a frog

Look at the peacock's tail,
What do you see?

I see a bursting volcano,
I see an exploding firework.

Melanie Sharpe (9)
Rushmere Hall Primary School, Ipswich

A Peacock's Tail

In a peacock's tail I can see . . .
Red, as red as a fire extinguisher,
Green, as green as a lily pad,
Black, as black as frogs spawn,
Blue, as blue as a dark whale.

Like a red tomato
Like a green cucumber
Like a black beetle
Like a blue dolphin

Look at a peacock's tail, what do you see?
I see a nest in front of me.

Chloe Gordon (9)
Rushmere Hall Primary School, Ipswich

A Peacock's Tail

In a peacock's tail I can see . . .

Red, as red as roses
Blue, as blue as blueberries
Purple, as purple as lavender.

Like a rose
Like a snowflake
Like lavender

Look at a peacock's tail, what can you see?
I see loads of eyes, a burst of red roses
I see a cold breeze of a snowflakes
Also a purple smell of lavender.

Hannah Leek (9)
Rushmere Hall Primary School, Ipswich

Birds Of Prey

Birds of prey live near the bay
To feed on fish and bits of clay.
They play with the rats
Watched by the bats
Who scares it away
With one quick flash
The rat comes back
Wearing its mac
The rain comes now
So the bat decides to bow
The sun shines bright
So they have a little fight
The rat beats the bat
And has a little nap
Along comes a cat
And eats the fat rat.

Sophie Campbell (9)
Rushmere Hall Primary School, Ipswich

Autumn

Summer's falling, autumn's calling,
Colours forming, leaves are falling,
Global warming, Nature's warning,
While summer's falling and autumn's calling
Time is flying!

Prakash Modasia (10)
Rushmere Hall Primary School, Ipswich

The Garden Fairy

Her wings like silver
Her heart like gold
Her warm blue eyes
Are bright and bold

Her petal dress
Past her knees
She drinks honey
Straight from the bees

Her wings are as dainty
As a spider's home
She's never without
Her golden comb

Her skin is as
Pale as icy snow
But she brings
Happiness wherever she goes

Her wings like silver
Her heart like gold
She holds a story
Never told.

Imogen Clarke (11)
Rushmere Hall Primary School, Ipswich

I Used To Rule The World

I used to rule the world
The crops would harvest themselves
The houses would clean themselves
The flowers would bloom just like that
All on my command

I used to rule the world
The seas would rise
Night would fall
The rain would start and stop
All on my command

I used to rule the world
The clocks would set themselves
The clothes would hang all by themselves
The sunrise and sunset would rise and fall
All on my command

I used to rule the world
Now I must wait for flowers to bloom
Wait for the rain to stop
Wait for the sunrise and sunset to rise and fall
Now, I don't rule the world

I used to rule the world
Now I must hang the clothes
Now, set the clocks myself
Now, clean the house myself
Now, I don't rule the world

I used to rule the world
Now I must harvest the crops myself
Now I must wait for night to fall
I can't make the seas rise
Now I don't rule the world.

Tilly Crowhurst (10)
Rushmere Hall Primary School, Ipswich

A Peacock's Tail

In a peacock's tail I can see
Green, as green as a bush
Yellow, as yellow as a lemon
Blue, as blue as the sky
Like a daffodil
Like a cabbage
Like the sky
Look at the peacock's tail
What do you se . . .
The colours of a rainbow.

Jordan Flude (9)
Rushmere Hall Primary School, Ipswich

A Peacock's Tail

In a peacock's tail I can see . . .
As red as a hall of rubies
As blue as a whale
As red as a rushing comet
As blue as the sea

Red like a strawberry
Blue like the ocean
Red like a holly berry
Blue like a rushing wave

In a peacock's tail I can see . . .

I can see a red firework
Circling around blue dazzling eyes.

I can see red fiery eyes.

Toby Ashbee (9)
Rushmere Hall Primary School, Ipswich

A Peacock's Tail

In a peacock's tail I see . . .
Red, as red as strawberries
Green, as green as pears
Purple, as purple as juicy plums

Like apples
Like bushes
Like Ribena

Look at the peacock's tail, what do you see?
I see thousands of eyes.

Jonathan Ferris (9)
Rushmere Hall Primary School, Ipswich

Once Upon A Time

Once upon a time in Royal Land,
lived a skinny, old wizard with a wand in his hand.
Potions, spells and a cauldron too,
it's dangerous for me and it's dangerous for you.

Until one day there was an idea,
'No more wizard!' cried a boy with no fear.
'Take his potion, his spells and his cauldron too,
it will be peaceful for me and peaceful for you.'

And that was the plan from that day on,
the potions, the spells, they were all gone.

Abigail Page (11)
St Augustine of Canterbury Primary School, Gillingham

Battles

B attles we have there is no need.
A nd sometimes it is over greed.
T he battles we have need to stop, stop, stop.
T error spreads across the land.
L et's not let it expand.
E veryone we should not fight.
S tart again and get it right.

Jake Turner (10)
St Augustine of Canterbury Primary School, Gillingham

A Frozen Battle

In the distance of the mist,
Fairy queens order pixies to scatter dust,
A warlock at the top of a castle creating prize potions,
The king counts men as he prepares for battle.
A troll under the bridge where the galloping goat stands,
He runs as a gigantic rock soars through the air,
The catapults are ready and the battle has started,
Smish! Smash! Crish! Crash!
Whom shall win?

Several warriors lose their lives,
Crowds appear everywhere,
Trees stare, clouds glare, everyone stops to watch.
The warlock drops his potion out of the window,
The battle stops,
Everyone is friends again,
Now this is how I say . . .
. . . The end.

Kirsty Verrent (10)
St Augustine of Canterbury Primary School, Gillingham

Once Upon A Time

Cinderella met a nice fella
Red Riding Hood ate all my pud
Sleeping Beauty is a cutey
Emperor's new clothes, get washed with a hose
Dear Princess Jasmine loves her old cat Tasmin
Big Bad Wolf gets kicked with a horses hoof
My land, my dream, they go on and gleam.

Natasha Udu (10)
St Augustine of Canterbury Primary School, Gillingham

My Best Friends Rule

Ellie is an ogre who patrols the land,
If you cross her path she will become mad,
Unless you come at noon to the port,
While she watches the weather report.

June is a dinosaur
If you come near her hear her fearsome roar,
The only way to get far,
Is to give her a chocolate bar.

Millie is a one-handed troll and the ugliest of the land,
But is the first to get a nice man,
If you're not a fool,
You will bring her some gruel.

Natasha is a cheeky monkey,
But is rather funky,
She likes to party,
And is rather laughy.

Kirsty is a baboon,
And rather a loon,
She is the first to get a phone,
But would rather find a bone.

Amber MacGregor (10)
St Augustine of Canterbury Primary School, Gillingham

Canvies Castle

I lay at the top of Canvies Castle,
Waiting for someone to rescue me,
All I'm allowed to drink is a cup of tea,
Downstairs all I hear is she, she, she,
It's time for a horrible dinner,
I can tell you when dinner comes,
No one's full of glee,
One cloudy night I heard a noise,
I woke up and there he stood,
A handsome young prince,
I was in my own land,
From that day onwards we had
an exciting life,
We love each other very much.

Ellie Harding (11)
St Augustine of Canterbury Primary School, Gillingham

Dragons

Once upon a time there was a dangerous daring dragon,
Devouring everything in his way,
Everyone was shocked and always came to say,
'OK, we're taking the dragon away!'
The demon dragon didn't like this one bit,
Especially when they all cheered, 'Hooray!'
The dragon yelped, the dragon screamed,
Demanding, 'Please don't hurt me!'
The villagers thought,
The villagers seemed, to see no dragon and they were pleased.

The dragon had run away from them.
They were never to see him ever again.

Daisy Lukins (10)
St Augustine of Canterbury Primary School, Gillingham

Fairyland Queen

F airyland queen
A bove all fairies
R eading them like a book
I n her throne, fluttering around with her hook
Y ou are her fairy maid
L oving you like she loves me
A nd chattering about her fairyland tea
N ow she is showing us how to be a fairy queen
'D on't be rude,' Queen says

Q ueue up to see my queen
U nicorns, my dream
E nough beauty to suit herself
E veryone thinks she's a beauty
N ow go to sleep and wait until the morning.

Cheyenne Hepburn (11)
St Augustine of Canterbury Primary School, Gillingham

Winter Wonderland

Snow, snow, snow, everyone knows
This is the place to be.
Snowball fight, it's lovely playing snow angels.
Lovely stars coming out in the bright moonlight,
Now that's my cup of tea!
Or maybe ice hockey, it is luxury!
You can do anything you please,
Lovely snow glistening every day
Snow expands in the winter wonderland!

Bradley Williams (10)
St Augustine of Canterbury Primary School, Gillingham

The Witch

Once upon a time there was a green witch,
She had a frog, dogs, rats and her old black cat.
She grinned showing her great white teeth
That she polishes almost every day!
She cackles with joy so much I can tell you.
I tried and tried to get her to start crying instead of making her cat run away!
It would have been amazing to get her out of her home place
But she was worried all the people would run away.
So there we went, another day gone
I needed to run because there she came, after me for her tea.

Rachael Mancattelli (10)
St Augustine of Canterbury Primary School, Gillingham

The Tooth Fairy

Small not tall,
Some are late, some are great.
When it's night, off to their job they go,
Glide down the hallway, slide through the doorway.
Up to the bed, lift the child's head.
Under the pillow, lay the shiny white tooth.
Pull out the little silk bag, and place the tooth inside.
Then back to the palace, to show the great queen with pride.

June King (10)
St Augustine of Canterbury Primary School, Gillingham

Read The Book

Once upon a time,
I opened a book,
Turned the pages and had a look.
'Come with me my little honey,
I can get you lots of money.
Just say the words shrink dink,
It's an adventure for you I think.
Along the way you will meet:
A dragon, a goblin and a troll named Pete.
If you want to go back,
It's too late now,
You have to stay here with me for an hour!'

Millie Nunn (10)
St Augustine of Canterbury Primary School, Gillingham

Fantasy Books

Magicians, monsters and other creatures
All of these have different features.
Talking trees, goblins and ghouls
If you don't like fantasy you're surely a fool.
You have to admit fantasy's better than school.
If you read fantasy books, you're really cool!

Isaac Owen (11)
St Augustine of Canterbury Primary School, Gillingham

Fantasy

F antastic wizards, trolls and monsters
A nd fights and battles spread through the land
N on magical people watch in wonder
T error stricken through the land
A ttacks on the magical land
S ieges on castles and forts
Y elling warriors as they attack.

Nathan Page (11)
St Augustine of Canterbury Primary School, Gillingham

Dear Little Red Riding Hood . . .

'Why do you wear red?
Why is your grandma still in bed?
Did you give your grandma a big, bad bun?
Were you scared of the wolf, the big, bad one?
Were you scared about his teeth?
Does he smell like roast beef?
Has your grandma got a bad head?
Is the wolf dead?
I hope grandma likes the bread,
From 52 Fairytale Homestead.'

Ebony Cummins (7)
St Augustine's CE Junior School, Peterborough

Hey Remi

Who taught you to cook?
Did you look in a book?
What did you make?
Was it a cake?
Is your brother Emil?
Did you make an appeal?
Did you makes friends with a meany?
Was his name Linguine?
Are we coming to the end?
The restaurant is just round the bend.

Natalia Hutchings (7)
St Augustine's CE Junior School, Peterborough

Cindy . . .

Do you hate your ugly sisters?
Do they have warts and blisters?
Do they boss you around all day?
Do they never let you play?
Do they try to chop off your head?
Do they ever let you rest in bed?
Do they make you sweep and sweep?
Do they ever let you say a peep?
Do they lock you in your room?
Do you feel like you are doomed?
Do they put a bolt on your door?
Do your ugly sisters snore?
Do you hide a lot of things?
Do you hear your ugly sisters sing?
Are you glad you are now the princess?
You are finally out of that mess!

Lauren Ippolito (7)
St Augustine's CE Junior School, Peterborough

Hey Miss Cinderella . . .

How did you feel when you had to dress the Ugly Sisters for the ball?
How did you feel when the prince came to call?
What was it like when you danced all night?
When the clock struck 12 did you have a fright?
Did you lose your shoe on purpose or not?
When you danced with the prince did your heart beat a lot?
At your wedding who did sing?
Did the prince give you a beautiful ring?
Are you still married to the prince today?
Hooray!

Lucy Royle (7)
St Augustine's CE Junior School, Peterborough

Hey Giant . . .

Why did you eat Jack?
Why did Jack steal the golden sack?
Why did you shout, 'Fee fo fi fum?
I smell the blood of an Englishman?
Did you put Jack on a line to hang?
Did you like it when the gold harp sang?
Why did you buy the golden goose?
Do you drink a lot of carrot juice?
Are you still in the castle in the sky?
We want to know . . . why?

Alfie Anderson (7)
St Augustine's CE Junior School, Peterborough

Hey Big Bad Wolf . . .

What did you say to Little Red Riding Hood?
Did you see her in the wood?
Did you eat Grandma's food?
That's very rude!
What did you do to Little Red Riding Hood?
Did you hurt her in the wood?
Where did you get your big eyes?
Did you find them in the ice?
You looked funny in Grandma's clothes,
Were you really wearing a bow?
What did the woodcutter think?
Did he give you a sly wink?
Why are your teeth so white,
Did you brush them in the night?
Are you ten feet tall?
I think you're bigger than my wall!
Where did you run away to,
Do you now work in a zoo?
Have you ever gone fishing yet?
Did you catch yourself in a net?
Who told you about the house?
It is true, was it really a mouse?
I'm glad you're not dead!
Enough said!

Angel-Skye Hudson (7)
St Augustine's CE Junior School, Peterborough

Dear Reddy Riding Hood . . .

Why do you wear red?
Why is your grandma still in bed?
Has the wolf bumped his head?
Has grandma baked some terrific bread?
Does it make you sleep when you go to bed?
Is the wolf in Grandma's shed?
'Now Grandma is better
She's sitting in bed eating lots of bread,'
Whispered Little Reddy Riding Hood.

Ebonie Rhode (8)
St Augustine's CE Junior School, Peterborough

Treasure - Cinquain

Treasure
The chest lays still
Full up with golden rings
Buried in the sand money hides.
Treasure.

Fearn Short (11)
St Lawrence CE Primary School, Colchester

Ocean - Cinquain

Ocean
Dangerous waves,
Swirling, crashing, plunging,
Deep inside the whirlpool of Hell.
The death.

Isabella Hutton (10)
St Lawrence CE Primary School, Colchester

Treasure Island - Cinquain

Island
Blazing heatwave
Water and deep blue sea
Tropical storms, mosquito bites.
Dead meat.

Frank Bush (10)
St Lawrence CE Primary School, Colchester

Pirates - Haiku

Hellish-looking teeth,
Battle-scarred skin, tattered clothes,
Singing shanty songs.

Finley Hughes (10)
St Lawrence CE Primary School, Colchester

Treasure - Cinquain

Treasure
Silver money
Covered in green seaweed
The maps show you to destiny
Crystals.

Chloe Tatum (9)
St Lawrence CE Primary School, Colchester

Black Dog - Haiku

The disgusting man,
With a bird on his shoulder,
A patch on his eye.

Holly Went (10)
St Lawrence CE Primary School, Colchester

Island - Haiku

Golden, warming sand
Shaded by rough, green palm trees
Huge sun beating down.

Neave Lynes (11)
St Lawrence CE Primary School, Colchester

Pirates - Haiku

Deadly man drinking,
Not afraid of anything
In the seven seas.

Jordan Moncur (10)
St Lawrence CE Primary School, Colchester

Pirates

Noisy,
Treasure stealing,
One-legged and cold-hearted,
Drunken excuse of a man.
Pirates.

Cara Brackpool (10)
St Lawrence CE Primary School, Colchester

Treasure

Treasure,
Sabotaged lock,
Emeralds reflecting sun,
Marvelling money watching on,
Bounty.

Sean Sargent (10)
St Lawrence CE Primary School, Colchester

Pirate Ship - Haiku

Wooden planks tattered,
Skull and crossbones flying and
Ripped sails guide the way.

Georgia Scott (10)
St Lawrence CE Primary School, Colchester

Pirates - Haiku

Billy Bone's scarred face
Sailing across the water
Boarding people's ships.

Ewan Black (10)
St Lawrence CE Primary School, Colchester

Pirates - Haiku

Dangerous pirates
Pirates killing on the beach
Pirates are dying.

Jordan Mitchell (10)
St Lawrence CE Primary School, Colchester

Ocean - Haiku

Ocean, deep and blue,
Ship cruised over the ocean,
Crashed upon the rocks.

Thomas Dunningham (11)
St Lawrence CE Primary School, Colchester

Autumn

Misty Monday mornings
Leaves running across the muddy floor
Coldness racing across England
Conkers hitting the ground with a thump
It's night and the sun's gone to bed
Marshmallows being roasted like a human in the sun.

Megan Till (10)
St Lawrence CE Primary School, Colchester

Pirates - Haiku

Old, one-legged man
Sitting on his treasure chest
He's slowly gulping.

Joshua Tatum (11)
St Lawrence CE Primary School, Colchester

Lap Cat

Whiskers,
Sleek and shiny,
Searching for a warm place,
A furry ball for you to stroke.
Purring.

Katherine Mann (7)
The King's School, Ely

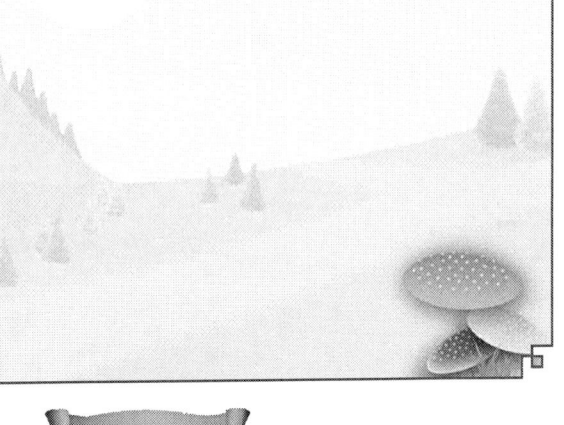

Autumn

A ll the leaves are falling to the ground,
U se the apples to make a pie,
T ake conkers home, fill your pockets till they burst,
U p in the sky the fireworks burst into bright colours,
M ake piles of leaves and one, two, three, jump in them,
N ow all the animals are hibernating.

Eleanor Wallace (8)
The King's School, Ely

Sweet Tooth

Sweets, sweets, lovely sweets
I went to a sweet shop and I saw lollipops,
Candy canes and fizzy drops.
Did I mention I have a sweet tooth?
Sweets, they are so good for you - oh no they're not.
They make your teeth rot . . .

India Thomas (8)
The King's School, Ely

I Know A Witch

I know a witch who has a black cat.
I know a witch who has a werewolf.
I know a witch who drives a broomstick.
I know a witch who has an owl.

Her cat lives in her huge black hat.
Her werewolf lives in the great, spooky hall.
Her broomstick lives in the creepy cobwebs.
Her owl lives in a fluffy towel.

Izzy McMillan (7)
The King's School, Ely

After Death

As I sail across the seas,
I say life is like a spiral
And when it stops, suddenly
You get kicked off the Earth,
You fall into a pit,
The water starts to shape into sand,
Flat sand. a table appears,
Five men in white cloaks, one with a black cloak
Are holding a big book with sins
And the good things you have said and done in your life.
You go up in the air or down into the pit.

Lucky Daniel Pogoson (7)
The King's School, Ely

A Nightly Visitor

From pink, naked and small
To a prickly, round ball
Explores my garden at night
Gave my dog a fright!

Snuffle, grunt, snuffle grunt
Through the undergrowth you do shunt
I hear you before I see you
My torch locates you as you come into view

You eat my cat food and drink my water
Beware of my pond though or hedgehog slaughter!
We know you can swim but soon reach the heather
We have installed a ramp to assist your endeavour

Jet-black eyes, cute pink nose
Sharp claws at the end of your toes
You love eating slugs and other garden pests
You ensure my vegetables are the best

I love your hoglets
Sweet little sproglets
My garden is now hedgehog proof
As long as you can't climb on our roof!

Jasmine Choudhry (9)
The King's School, Ely

My Sister Emily

Emily likes a teddy bear,
She likes some reading too,
Emily has long, brownish hair
And eyes of greyish blue.

My sister swims just like a frog
And runs just like a deer,
She's scared of even tiny dogs,
But rabbits bring no fear.

My sister dances like a loon,
She always bosses me,
She likes a film that's called 'New Moon'
That we don't agree.

She's funny, clever and my mate
I'm glad that we're sisters, *great!*

Bethany Thorpe (10)
The King's School, Ely

Halloween

Boo! I scared you like a fool,
To rule Halloween
Because you are not the Queen
You're just mean
When you're in a mood
Don't eat your food!
When it's Halloween just run and scream!

Isabelle Jupp (8)
The King's School, Ely

Shem

Shem, our black and white cat is old,
But doesn't know it, he plays like a kitten,
Jumping for scrunched up balls of paper,
Like a goalkeeper.

He can climb like a panther
And likes to hang upside down
In my dad's arms,
But sometimes gets stuck in the big apple tree
And cries like a baby.

He prefers an old cardboard box to a basket,
Sleeps on a radiator until he's too hot
And jumps off with a cry,
Likes to leave his fleas on our blankets
And has fluorescent eyes.

In a bad mood he will hiss
And drag his drinking bowl around when it's empty,
He hates loud noise, the wind and jazz,
He misses his old friend, our lurcher, Sombra.
Shem came running to me once
At the sound of the old dead dog's collar.

He has caught every kind of bird,
(Very bad!) as well as voles and mice,
But a blackbird still comes into our house.
Now that he's old, he likes best
To curl up warm on my lap,
In his nest.

Aurora Segre Carnell (7)
The King's School, Ely

Leaks

Now the rain comes pouring downwards
Pitter patter overhead
It leaks in through the rusty pipes
As you sit up in your bed

Dripping, dropping water comes
Splashing on the bathroom floor
Sneaking through the tiny cracks
As you watch it leave its tracks

You dab the water with a towel
But more keeps weeping from the roof
You slosh your feet through some big puddles
And watch your bathroom slowly drown

You creep downstairs to see the damage
But not a lot has happened there
But then your heart clunks in your chest
As the ceiling starts to leak

Soon the kitchen joins the fun
And tiny puddles start to form
But then a smile steals your face
As with the morning comes the sun

The water tries to hide and run
But nothing can evade the sun
You kit out with a sponge and cloth
And help the sun dry your house

Soon your house is barely damp
And you yawn with sleepiness
You realise you did not sleep
As you jump into your bed

The next day you fix up the entire house
And it's all because of leaks.

Hannah Okechukwu (10)
The King's School, Ely

Lemon Cake

Lemon cake is sweet and sour
The only one you could wish for hours

Cheesecake and muffins are not the ones
But lemon cake is another one

Teachers and children love it
Maybe will have to make more of it

I could have it for breakfast
I could have it for dinner
Maybe it's a winner

I could go for hours eating lemon cake
But the best part is to actually bake the cake

I really do love lemon cake
But I think I have got a bit of a stomach ache!

Darcie Jupp (10)
The King's School, Ely

Music

How does music make me feel
When I hear its beautiful sound?
I think and wonder of unimaginable things.
Music takes me to another world beyond this galaxy,
A world of sound and wonder.
Music gives me lots of things, happiness, ideas and my *life!*

James Hinton (10)
The King's School, Ely

More Disobedience
(Based on 'Disobedience' by Alan Alexander Milne, 1882-1956)

James James
Morrison Morrison
Weatherby George Dupree
Took great care of his mother
Though he was only three.
James James
Said to his mother,
'Mother,' he said, said he,
'You must never go on the Internet,
Without consulting me.'

James James
Morrsion's mother
Clicked www.dot
James James
Morrison's mother
Began to click a lot.
James James
Morrison's mother
Said to herself, said she,
'I'll just see if I can find
Some lovely treats for tea.'

James James
Morrison's mother
Bought a pasta to bake.
James James
Morrison's mother
Found a ginger cake.
A few clicks more and rings on the door,
She soon had parcels all over the floor.

James James
Morrison's mother
Purchased a golden gown
James James
Morrison's mother
Bought a car to get into town.
James James
Morrison's mother
Clicked on Happy Bets,
James James
Morrison's mother
Started to get debts.

James James
Morrison's mother
Was put in a prison cell,
James James
Morrison's mother
Said to James, 'Farewell.'
James James
Morrison's mother
Said to herself, said she
'I must never go on the Internet
Without consulting he.'

James James
Morrison Morrison
(commonly known as Jim)
Told his friends and relations
Not to go blaming him.
James James
Said to his mother,
'Mother,' he said, 'Yahoo.
If people go clicking all over the place
Well, what can anyone do?'

Katie Diss (10)
The King's School, Ely

The Secret Garden

Once there was a garden,
A beautiful garden with honeysuckle on the gate.
It is a secret because a unicorn found it.
Wow! Wow! I can't believe he invited me to tea in the garden!
Wow! I can't shut my eyes because it's so beautiful.
I love it, I love it, so let me describe it . . .

It has a band and a disco,
It also has roses on the wall and rows and rows of silver bells.
It has a swimming pool,
It also has a water fountain so small.

Erin Ilma Carney (7)
The Westborough School, Westcliff-on-Sea

Rainbow, Rainbow

Rainbow, Rainbow, you are so bright,
Beautiful colours all so bright,
Reds and pinks,
Blues and greens,
Lots of colours, they all gleam.

Sharna Gosling (7)
The Westborough School, Westcliff-on-Sea

RHYME – Poems From The East

Animals

Animals are so cute
Animals are so funny
I like their stripes
I like their patterns
I like their colours
I like their style
I like their fur
I like their voices
I like their life.

Molly Tudor (7)
The Westborough School, Westcliff-on-Sea

Autumn

I can smell the fresh grass and it is prickly and long,
I can hear the leaves crackling in my ear like thunder.
I can feel the tree bark, it is so rough.
I can see the leaves and they are folding up.
I can touch the leaves and they are prickly.

Anne-Marie Ewing (7)
Welbourne Primary School, Peterborough

Football Crazy

Football crazy, football mad
I play football with my dad
I like to play in the house
But Mum gets very cross
Me and Dad get in trouble
With her, because she's the boss
Over eight hundred football cards
A very big collection
Some of them are very shiny
They give a reflection
Dad took me to my first match
Sunderland versus Posh
There were lots of people at the ground
Good job I wasn't squashed
Dad and me like watching football
On our flat screen telly
Dad cheers loud when they score
I sit and eat my jelly
Football crazy, football mad
The best times I spend with my dad.

Charlie Orbell (7)
Welbourne Primary School, Peterborough

Let's Go Outside

Let's go outside
Skipping together
Having fun
Friends laughing
And playing
In the sun
It's shining in
My face
Let's go outside
It's nice and sunny
All the leaves
Are curling now
It's calm
Blackberries
Are growing
Time to pick
With you
It's nice
Outside,
Let's go outside.

Karis Adams (7)
Welbourne Primary School, Peterborough

Let's Go Outside

Let's go outside and explore
Look, I see a crunchy leaf
And tree leaves waving
And children playing.
The wind is blowing
The sun is shining in the sky
The wind is getting stronger
The acorns are falling really fast
The clouds are whispering
The birds are singing to the sky.

Owen Reed (7)
Welbourne Primary School, Peterborough

Let's Go Outside

The sun is yellow, the wind is blowing
The leaves, the brown leaves,
The birds flying the sky is blue,
The grass is spiky, soft, wet grass,
I hear cars, wind, children,
I smell mud and nothing.

Erikas Grigutis (7)
Welbourne Primary School, Peterborough

Let's Go Outside

The wind is blowing
The grass is green
I can see the park
I can see children
I can see the school
I can smell the grass
I can hear the aeroplane
I can see a cross
I can see trees and leaves.

David Cruz (7)
Welbourne Primary School, Peterborough

Let's Go Outside

Let's go outside,
The wind is blowing in the air,
The grass is prickly and is long,
I can see the brown leaves,
I can see the grass,
I can see the aeroplane,
I can see the clouds making an X,
I can see the play park,
I can feel the table banging like drums.

Brandon Bonner (7)
Welbourne Primary School, Peterborough

Autumn

In the autumn
Leaves fall from the trees
In the colours of red, orange
Yellow and brown
As the wind blows through the trees
It makes me feel calm and chilly
As I walk the leaves crunch under my feet
But in my hands feel soft and smooth.

Caery Brandreth (7)
Welbourne Primary School, Peterborough

Let's Go Outside

The wind is blowing in the air
The leaves are brown.
The trees are swaying
People are playing.
The wind keeps blowing my paper!

Jacob Thompson
Welbourne Primary School, Peterborough

Let's Go Outside

The leaves are all around me,
I can hear the cars.
The smell of wood,
Children are playing.
I can see the train track and the trees
And a red slide and a climbing frame.
The sun is shining,
I feel the wind is all around me.
Planes are flying
And rainbow colours are all around the world.
Special things around me.

Daria Slaby (7)
Welbourne Primary School, Peterborough

I Saw . . .

I saw the bright, white snow
I saw how quickly the sledges go
I saw the people in matching scarves and gloves
I saw, up in a tree, two snuggled doves
I saw a snowball go by
I saw the angry victim cry
I saw some children decorating a snowman's head
I saw an old lady feeding the ducks with some bread
I saw some icicles glistening in the afternoon sun
I saw rosy-nosed children heading home after a busy day's fun!

Mia Thomsett-Hurrell (10)
Wicklewood Primary School, Wymondham

I Saw . . .

I saw a carrot eat a rabbit
I saw a giant apple with a nasty habit
I saw a coffee drink a man
I saw a hat wearing its woman
I saw a mouse hunt a cat
I saw a pig making a hat
I saw a pig wearing a wig
I saw a dog dance a jig!

Thomas Marshall (10)
Wicklewood Primary School, Wymondham

I Saw . . .

I saw a cloud eating candyfloss.
I saw a star using lipgloss.
I saw a hailstone crying.
I saw a clear sky dying.
I saw a sunbeam humming.
I saw a thunderstorm coming.
I saw a fiery comet crash into Mars.
I saw a strike of lightning hit lots of cars.
I saw icy skies.
I saw the moon's eyes.

Kirstin Angus (10)
Wicklewood Primary School, Wymondham

The Turnip

It pulled itself from under the ground,
All dirty.
It emerged among the muddy leaves,
Yearning never to be eaten.
Slowly a silhouette of something formidable
Zoomed into view,
The turnip quickly pulled on a top
And some shorts
And ran,
Only hoping to be safe!

Katie Ellen King (10)
Wicklewood Primary School, Wymondham

I Saw . . .

I saw a wolf with a threatening howl,
I saw a glossy feather from a big white owl,
I saw the trees with fiery red leaves,
I saw a princess with glittering white sleeves,
I saw a dragon with green, scaly skin,
I saw a flexible cat leap over the bin,
I saw a puppy with white, fluffy fur,
I saw a black and white cat that went purr!
I saw a lion with a big, golden mane,
I saw the children splash about in the pouring rain,
I saw a leopard with sugar-brown spots,
I saw a girl pouring paint in her bright pink pots.

Molly Young (10)
Wicklewood Primary School, Wymondham

I Saw . . .

I saw a gigantic pyramid made of gold,
I saw a scarlet-red dragon being sold,
I saw a wizard turn himself into a slimy green frog,
I saw a headless, pitch-black crocodile in the bog.
I saw a witch with a thousand bursting boils on her face,
I saw a huge van saying, *Go Away, This Is Now Monster's Place.*
I saw a hedgehog with the sharpest prickles in the land,
I saw a concert with noisiest band.
I saw a needle as sharp as knife,
I saw I had no life . . .
I saw my small, tiny friend,
I saw the Earth was coming to an end.

Phoebe Burton-White (10)
Wicklewood Primary School, Wymondham

I Saw . . .

I saw an eagle at blazing speed,
I saw a man with hunger and greed,
I saw a car with fixed red wheels,
I saw a beach with tonnes of seals,
I saw a cat encased by the night,
I saw a boxer prepared for a fight,
I saw a girl, so scared she could cry,
I saw a fox, so careful and sly,
I saw a rocket soar up to the moon,
I saw a flower just starting to bloom,
I saw a friend coming to say 'Hi,'
After we played we then said, 'Goodbye!'

Dominic Cohen (11)
Wicklewood Primary School, Wymondham

Lost For Words

Slowly letter *S* came into view walking up the stairs on the brain,
Next moment, *puff*, the word had gone.
Slowly, letters *C* and *A* walked up, but then slowly vanished.

Wait . . .

Next, letter *R* came and unfortunately decide to take the short cut through the ear but just ended up walking out the other.

Wait . . .

Then *E* cheerily walked up the first step into the head
And just fell back down again.

Wait . . .

Suddenly, brave *D* appeared in the centre of the brain.
So in the end, after all that pain, they had a word!

Scared!

Catherine Jones (10)
Wicklewood Primary School, Wymondham

Blank Mind

My mind is blank
My mind is bare
With only one word
I cannot spare.
As it dies slowly
Then it drifts into the air.
A bare, empty mind
I can't help it!
It feels like all my ideas
Have fallen into a deep, dark pit.
I try to think, but it doesn't work
My thoughts stopped working . . .

Rebekah Devlin (10)
Wicklewood Primary School, Wymondham

My Brain Has Died

Brainless and blank
My brain has fallen asleep
And won't wake up.

I look around
Everyone has written
A page or two.
I get my papers, saying
'Oh no, here it comes, ah, I have torn in half!'
No joke, I think my brain has died!
It's in one ear and out the other.
As soon as the word looked at me it ran away,
And here we go,
My page is blank
Five minutes left
Two minutes left
'Put down you pens and stop writing.'
The teacher's flicking through my book
She's found my work
What happens next?

Tonita Holloway (10)
Wicklewood Primary School, Wymondham

Empty Head

Nothing in my head
But I know there's an idea, ready to pounce
Ready to attack
Ready to bounce!
My brain said, 'Help.'
My pen said 'No!'
I had it for a little while
A moment ago!
But then it vanished
It went away
Never to be heard of
On any other day!

Luke Custance (10)
Wicklewood Primary School, Wymondham

Creatures

There are
Giant ones
Cuddly ones
Strict ones
One that hide in bushes ones
Flying ones
Scaly ones
Scary ones
Ones that died in the Ice Age ones
Microscopic ones
Silky ones
Happy ones
Friendly ones
Small ones
Ones that live in the forest ones.

Helena Imogen Geere (11)
Wicklewood Primary School, Wymondham

Quack

I have a yellow duck
Who likes to try his luck
He says quack which makes me jump
And when he waddles he looks a bit of a lump

My duck likes to race
All over the place
His name is Speedy
And he is very greedy

Speedy likes to eat Sugar Puffs, the milk he likes to lap
I just wish that sometimes he would just take a nap.

Toby Dunn (8)
Wicklewood Primary School, Wymondham

Brainless

My eyes keep staring at a blank page,
Er, umm, I can't think of what to write!
Help! I've so much to write and no time,
I'm brainless, blank, I've got an empty head.
I feel like I'm staring into an empty cupboard,
There's nothing there.
In my head time is as fast as the beat of a drum.
I am surrounded by lots of busy children,
Who have nearly finished!
Then there's me who's brainless,
Worried that my short piece of work is wrong.

Maria Shepherd (10)
Wicklewood Primary School, Wymondham

I Saw . . .

I saw a ferocious dog with six legs
I saw a linen line with multicoloured pegs
I saw a boy who looked like me
I saw a cat quickly climb a tree
I saw a car speeding down the road
I saw a really great big toad
I saw lightning flash at night
I saw a soldier deep in fight
I saw the hot and blazing sun
I saw a mouth-watering hot cross bun.

Harry Snook (10)
Wicklewood Primary School, Wymondham

My Dog, Pelly

Playful Pelly,
As cute as a button,
As naughty as a rascal,
Barks like a wolf,
But is as soft as a kitten,
Fur like shimmering silk,
Black and strong,
It's like her paws have been dipped in milk,
Eats like a piglet, with her teeth like white mountains,
She is very excitable and full of fun
And always pleased to see me,
I know so well, my beautiful Pell.

Anya Grace Droppert (10)
Wicklewood Primary School, Wymondham

I Saw . . .

I saw a crane as high as the sky
I saw a plane doing a stunt fly-by
I saw a New York taxi, it was bright yellow
I saw my home, all covered in marshmallow
I saw a big, green snake
I saw a massive Victoria sponge cake
I saw a spider as big as a plate
I saw a beetle crawling up the garden gate.

Owen Sully (10)
Wicklewood Primary School, Wymondham

Myths And Legends

A knight may dare to go into a dragon's lair!
He would draw his sword, but not call for the earth lord!
You know the dinosaurs, they didn't have little doggie paws!
You know the Romans, they weren't known as showmen!
Also the Greeks were known as freaks!
The Celts never wore belts!
I must tell you about the Normans, they were known as doormen!
There were also the Victorians and Edwardians.
Charles II loved to party, but he was not very arty!
Henry VIII loved to behead, but he didn't know about this fancy lead!

Lewis Saunders (8)
Wicklewood Primary School, Wymondham

Ellie's Poem

L ittle and lively
A dorable and sweet
B right and bouncy
R ight to her feet
A lways wagging her short tail
D oing her best to please
O n my lap she goes to sleep
O n the lead she scrapes her feet
D igging and playing she enjoys so much
L oves her food to fill her up
E llie's her name and she knows it well

    She's a Labradoodle, can't you tell?

Samantha Osborne (9)
Wicklewood Primary School, Wymondham

Corn

Corn stalks in a field of gold,
With nothing to do
But wait and hope.

Standing in the wind,
Whispers of freedom,
'Freedom, freedom.'

Softly and calmly
Pushing the corn stalks,
Left and right, left and right.

Suddenly the clouds grow grey,
And the sky becomes angry,
A flash of lightning stabs the corn.

Dark as night,
The corn slowly falls,
Down,
Down,
Down.

Ashley Bishop (10)
Wicklewood Primary School, Wymondham

My Idea

I had an idea in my head for my homework
And I was walking downstairs and then,
My brother hit me round the head
And my idea fell away.
So I thought really hard
And my idea came back again.

Lauryn Peacock
Worsley Bridge Junior School, Beckenham

An Idea Came Into My Head

An idea came into my head,
It was popping in and out of my head.
Next thing you know, all of sudden
It's in the air, floating like a delicate balloon.

An idea came into my head,
It was rushing in and out of my head,
Like a speedy river flowing,
Unfortunately leaving a little drop behind.

An idea came into my head,
It was booming in and out of my head,
Like a banging drum,
It left an echoing sound.

An idea came into my head,
In a flash flew straight into my head,
Like an enormous blue train.

An idea came into my head,
So tender, so sweet,
An idea came into my head.

Suzannah Ogunleye (10)
Worsley Bridge Junior School, Beckenham

When I'm On Holiday

When I'm on holiday I hear the sea and the sand whispers to me.
The warmth speaks in its calm voice then drifts off.

The sun shoots light bullets,
But then the moon and his shiny guards take over.
But in the morning the sun has reloaded,
But I have to say goodbye.

George Barrett (10)
Worsley Bridge Junior School, Beckenham

Crazy Idea

An idea drifts into my head and then pops like a bubble
And then a crazy idea comes to me.
It flies right in and right out into someone else's head.
An idea zooms in like a rocket at full speed.
An idea is crazy, like forever it swirls, twirls, it spins, it wins,
Like a car in a race and then it goes.
Then a rocket zooms through my head
And a great big idea stepped right in
And never went away.

Teyam Goode (10)
Worsley Bridge Junior School, Beckenham

A Girl's Idea Flowing Across Her Head

When I get an idea it flies across my mind
It swivels right through my cheery head
Sometimes I forget my ideas
So much for my typical brain.

When I'm walking by my friend's house
I get a wonderful idea
My friend waves to me
Then I forget my idea.

When I forget my idea I feel so frustrated
But when I do remember my wonderful ideas, ideas, ideas, ideas
I will not forget my ideas any more.

Sacha Shiels (10)
Worsley Bridge Junior School, Beckenham

Ideas In And Out Of My Head

An idea went into my leprechaun's pot of gold
And out again like lightning
Then it came back again
And slipped through my head like a bar of soap,
Then it went away like the sun on a cloudy day
It bounced on a trampoline like a rabbit trying to find dinner.

Max Owen (10)
Worsley Bridge Junior School, Beckenham

When I Was In Bed

When I was in bed I had an idea
But then the radiator melted it away
Like a zooming car passing by.
Than I got another idea
Then the wind blew it away like an angry bull
Running at a man.
Suddenly I was working
And I came up with a great idea
And my head blew up
And my idea ran away.

Tyruss Mays (10)
Worsley Bridge Junior School, Beckenham

Changing

The thunder howls like a wolf
The lightning is as fantastic as a BMW
Hail drops like bombers in the Blitz

The rain walks along the countryside
The sun is as happy as everyone else
The mist blinds like my torch.

Luke Lawrence (10)
Worsley Bridge Junior School, Beckenham

School Clock

The clock ticks by
Like a boat on a still sea

The clock ticks by
Like the growing of a tree

The clock says to me
I am slowing down now
By five whole seconds
And you better believe it, wow!

The clock face turns round and round
He sits on a Ferris wheel that never ends.

Delaney Anne Brewster (10)
Worsley Bridge Junior School, Beckenham

Powerful Ideas

An idea begins it buzzes fiercely in my head
Like a rocket shooting off into space.

Ideas slipping on my hand
Like a bright yellow bar of soap trying to get away.

Ideas sprinting from side to side with boredom,
Ideas crashing and popping
And buzzing an whistling.
When my ideas go my brainpower gets low.
Sometimes is disappears
And my fear gets clearer
And clearer and clearer.
When it comes back I learn
A big fact,
Never to let it go again.
Sometimes it gets on a train,
Then I blame it on my brother
Who fills up with shame
And when it comes back I get a big smack,
Then I never let my ideas get away again!

Chloe Brown (10)
Worsley Bridge Junior School, Beckenham

Fashion Girl

The silky sleeves of the coat
Hang on the chair
As it swings it arms back and forth.

The fluttering skirt
Danced around on the dance floor
Like a little butterfly.

The glittering, jewelled dress
Shimmered happily
Like a diamond necklace.

The disco diva dress shone happily
As it moved about on the dance floor
Into the night.

Leah Purton (10)
Worsley Bridge Junior School, Beckenham

Ideas Come And Go

An idea begins,
It whistles in my head,
Then the idea whistles
Back to bed.
Another idea comes alive,
It buzzes in my head
Like bees in a beehive.
Another idea blazes in my brain
Like a rocket going to Spain,
There it is,
Another idea comes along
And shines like a star in the night.

Shannon Partleton (10)
Worsley Bridge Junior School, Beckenham

Ideas And Words

Ideas whirling through my head
Like glitter in the cold and nippy winter.
Words on my page are pouncing
Like a crazy cat!
Ideas sprinting through my mind.
Ideas slip through my fingers
Like golden sand on a warm, sunny beach.
Words jump on my crisp, white paper
Like they are jumping off Golden Gate Bridge in San Francisco.
Ideas running off my page
Faster than Olympic runner, Usain Bolt.
Words running faster
Than Roadrunner from Loony Toons.
Ideas bouncing around my head
Like they are on Spacehoppers.
Words prancing around
Like they are on pogo sticks.
Ideas running through my head
So fast, it's a big blur.
Ideas galloping through my head
Like they are on horseback.
Words singing so loud
They could be on Britain's Got Talent.
Oh no, my ideas went in the garden,
Words march outside the house
Like proud British soldiers.

Charley Anderson (10)
Worsley Bridge Junior School, Beckenham

An Idea That's Willing To Come Out

An idea that's willing to come out,
It jumps, screams and shouts.
It howls like a wolf,
With echoing noises.
But I haven't used it yet!
It carries on,
It wants to be used,
I need to catch it before I lose.
The idea gets frustrated,
It has given me a headache,
So it looks like I have woe.
So it slips away to someone else,
The idea that got so close.

Mia Calver (10)
Worsley Bridge Junior School, Beckenham

An Idea

An idea begins as it echoes into my head,
Ideas begin to twirl in my brain,
Like an elegant ballerina,
They spin around in my head
Like a really bouncy ball.

Words jumping up and down
Like a kangaroo.
Words fly in my brain
Like a speeding rocket.
Words zooming through my brain
As fast as they can.
Words slipping through my fingertips
Like sugar.
Next thing you know
They are fading away quickly,
Flying out of my brain.
They must have flown far away
Because they never came back!

Danielle Allen (10)
Worsley Bridge Junior School, Beckenham

The Idea

My head is hollow
My head is shallow
But when a rocket came zooming in
An idea came out.
It looked around and thought
It's a nice place
But after a day
It flew away.

Archie Palmer (10)
Worsley Bridge Junior School, Beckenham

Young Writers Information

We hope you have enjoyed reading this book - and that you will continue to enjoy it in the coming years.

If you like reading and writing poetry drop us a line, or give us a call, and we'll send you a free information pack.

Alternatively, if you would like to order further copies of this book or any of our other titles, then please give us a call or log onto our website at www.youngwriters.co.uk.

Young Writers Information
Remus House
Coltsfoot Drive
Peterborough
PE2 9BF
Tel: (01733) 890066
Fax: (01733) 313524

Email: info@youngwriters.co.uk

Shakespeare Quiz Answers

1. Stratford-upon-Avon **2.** Romeo and Juliet **3.** James I **4.** 18 **5.** The Tempest **6.** Regan, Cordelia and Goneril **7.** His wife **8.** Venice **9.** All's Well That Ends Well, As You Like It, The Comedy of Errors, Cymbeline, Love's Labour's Lost, Measure for Measure, The Merchant of Venice, The Merry Wives of Windsor, A Midsummer Night's Dream, Much Ado About Nothing, Pericles - Prince of Tyre, The Taming of the Shrew, The Tempest, Twelfth Night, The Two Gentlemen of Verona, Troilus & Cressida, The Winter's Tale **10.** Henry V **11.** Claire Danes **12.** Macbeth **13.** Hamlet **14.** Sonnet